The Basic Guide to Word Processing

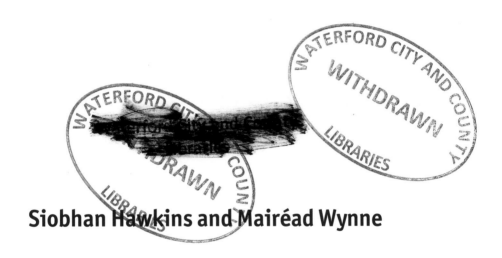

Siobhan Hawkins and Mairéad Wynne

Gill & Macmillan

Gill & Macmillan
Hume Avenue
Park West
Dublin 12

978 07171 4995 7

Print origination in Ireland by O'K Graphic Design, Dublin
Printed by GrapyCems, Spain

A CIP catalogue record for this book is available from the British Library.

CONTENTS

Unit 1 Microsoft Word 2010

Unit 3   Top Tips for Text Production

Unit 4 Exercises

QUICK ACCESS TOOLBAR

FILE TAB DROP MENU

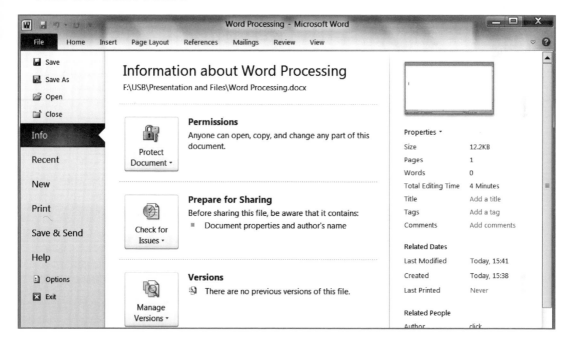

HOME TAB

INSERT TAB

PAGE LAYOUT TAB

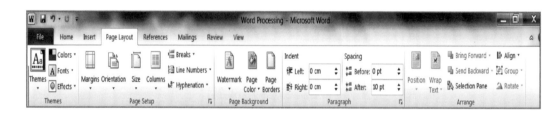

REFERENCES TAB

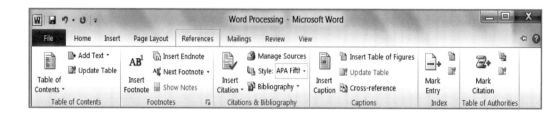

THE BASIC GUIDE TO WORD PROCESSING

MAILINGS TAB

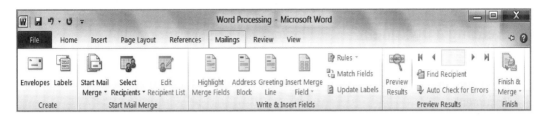

REVIEW TAB

VIEW TAB

1. FILE TAB MENU

Creating a Document

To create a new document, click on the FILE tab and select New. Then select Blank Document.

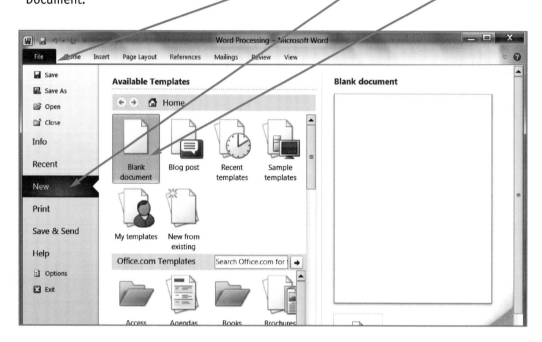

THE BASIC GUIDE TO WORD PROCESSING

Templates

To create and apply a template, simply click on the FILE tab and select New.

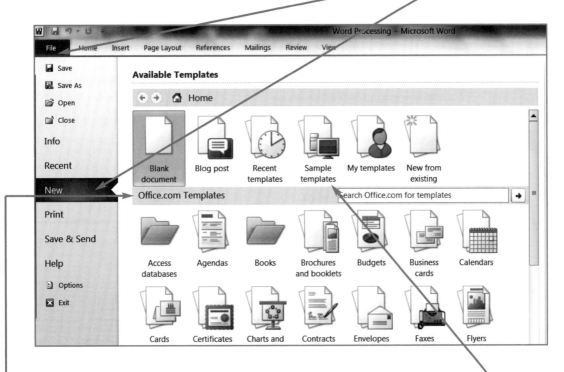

Then select from the Available Templates (some are installed on your computers – see Sample Templates, others are online and need internet access to use).

Save As

Save documents as: Document, Text File, web page etc.

1. To save your document, click on the FILE tab and select Save as.

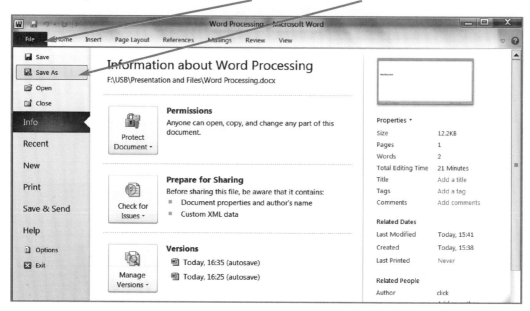

THE BASIC GUIDE TO WORD PROCESSING

2. The Save As window will open. Type in your file name.

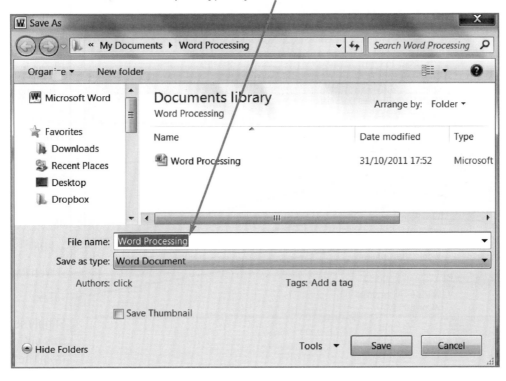

3. If you want to save your document as a text file, web page etc, select the Other Formats option.

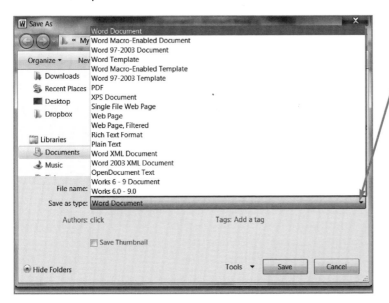

In the Save as Type section use the drop arrow to select the type of file you want to save your document as and click Save.

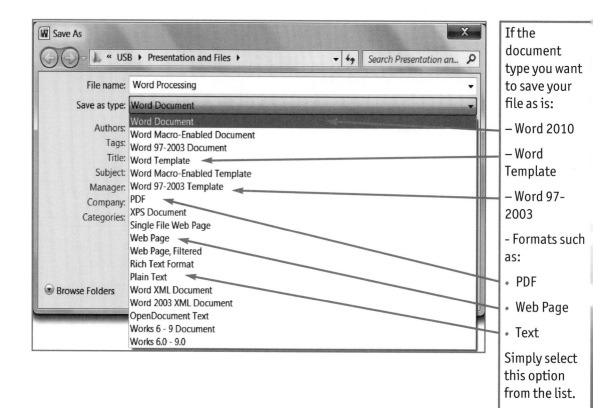

If the document type you want to save your file as is:

– Word 2010

– Word Template

– Word 97-2003

- Formats such as:

• PDF

• Web Page

• Text

Simply select this option from the list.

Print

Use a range of print features e.g. Print, Preview, print, Single / multiple copies, Print specific pages.

To print your document, click on the FILE tab and select Print.

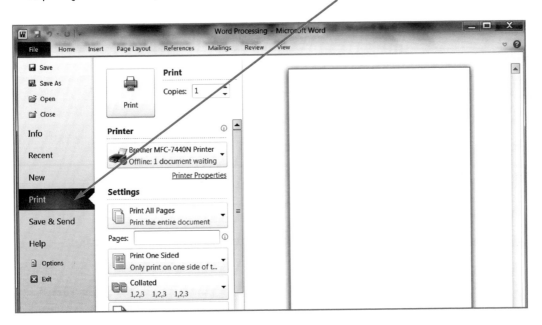

To preview your documents before printing them, use the Print Preview pane on the right-hand side.

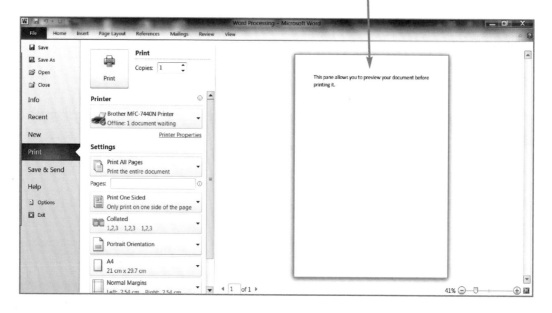

To print your document, click on Print and the Printer options screen will appear.

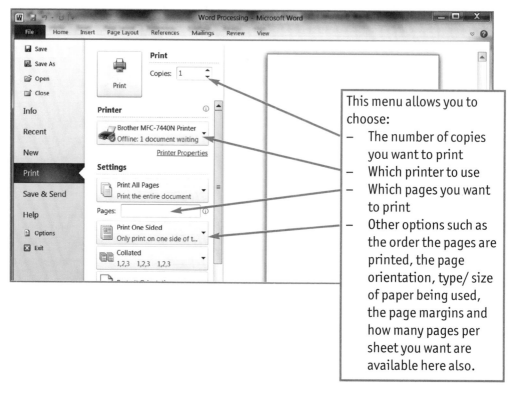

This menu allows you to choose:
- The number of copies you want to print
- Which printer to use
- Which pages you want to print
- Other options such as the order the pages are printed, the page orientation, type/ size of paper being used, the page margins and how many pages per sheet you want are available here also.

Properties such as colour/black and white printing, paper layout, paper size and quality of print can be changed by clicking on the Printer Properties button.

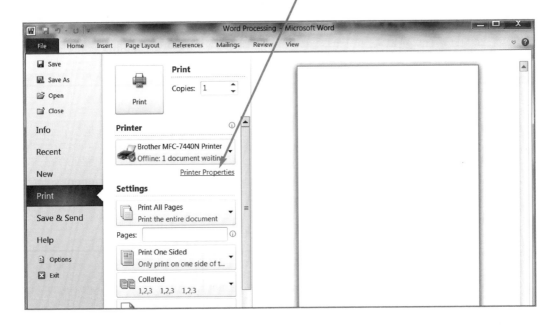

2. HOME TAB

Clipboard Section

Cut, Copy and Paste

Highlight the text you want to cut or copy.
In the Clipboard section of the HOME tab click Cut or Copy. Then, in your document select where you want to copy the information to and click Paste.

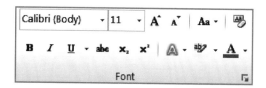

Text, images etc can be copied to a different section in the same document or copied into a different document.

Font Section

Making Text Bold, *Italic*, <u>Underlined</u> and Colour

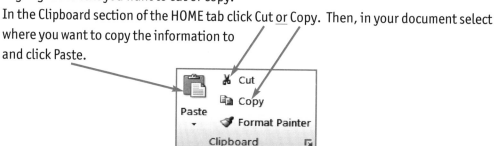

Click on the HOME tab. Highlight the text to format.

To make text **bold,** click on the **Bold** icon on the FORMATTING toolbar.

To make text *italic,* click on the *Italics* icon on the FORMATTING toolbar.

To <u>underline</u> text, click on the <u>Underline</u> icon on the FORMATTING toolbar.

Use the drop-down arrow to view different options.

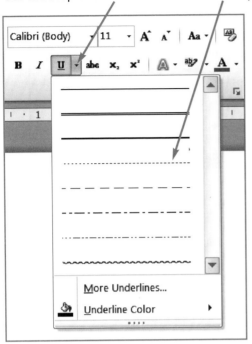

To put the text into colour, click on the 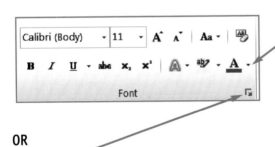 and use the drop-down arrow to select the colour.

OR

Click on the arrow on the Font bar.

needed under Font style.

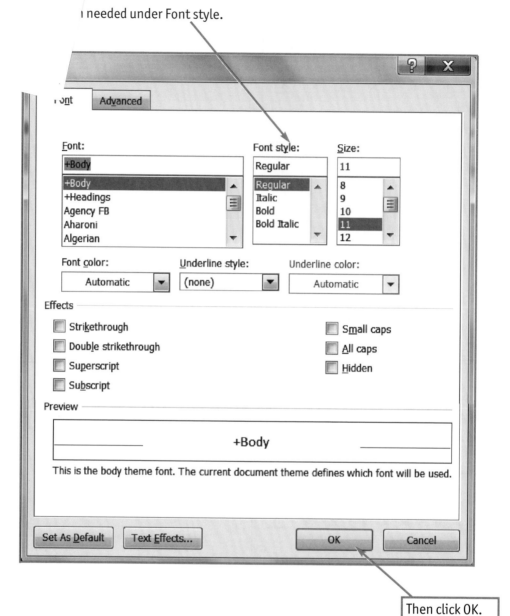

Then click OK.

Font Size

Click on the Font section of the HOME tab. Highlight the text where you want to change the font size. Click on the font size icon on the FORMATTING toolbar, click on the drop-down arrow and select the number you want to set your font size.

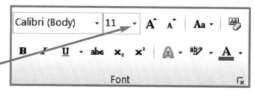

Font Effects 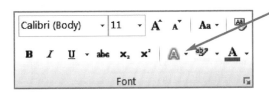 (Outline, Shadow, Reflection, Glow)

To add a visual effect to the text using different options, highlight the text you want to use the effect on and select the drop-down arrow on the Text Effect icon

Click on the effect you want to use.

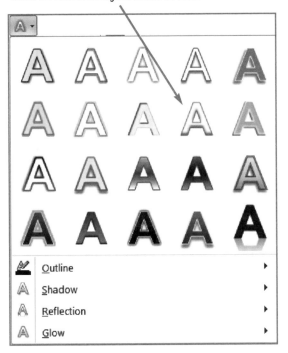

OR

Highlight the text you want to use the text effects on. Click on the arrow on the Font bar.

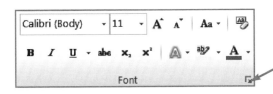

In the Effects section choose the effects you want use on your text.

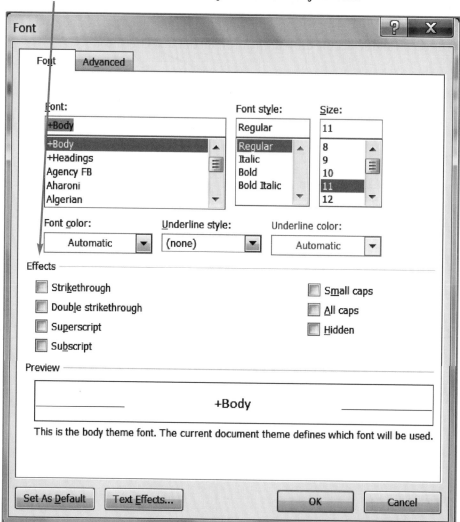

THE BASIC GUIDE TO WORD PROCESSING

CAPITALS

Highlight the text to be put in capitals. Under the HOME tab click on 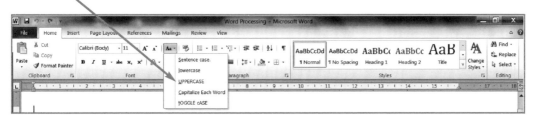 and select UPPERCASE.

Note: This can also be used to change UPPERCASE to lowercase, to tOOGLE cASE and to Capitalize Each Word (Initial Capitals).

Paragraph Section
Bullets and Numbering

To add bullets to existing text, select the text to which you want to add bullets. Add bullets by clicking on the bullets icon  on the Paragraph section under the HOME tab.

To choose a different format for the bullets, use the drop-down arrow beside the bullet icon 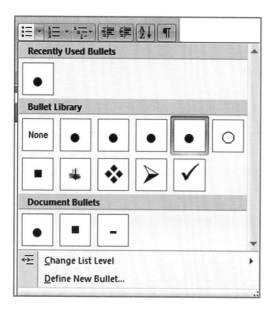 and click on the bullet format you want.

To remove bullets, select the text from which you want to remove bullets. Click on the bullets icon on the toolbar and the bullets are removed.

To add numbering, select the text to which you want to add numbering. Add numbering by clicking the numbers icon 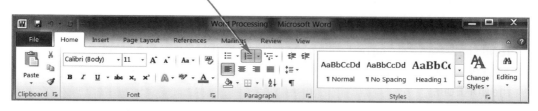 on the Paragraph section under the HOME tab.

To choose a different format for the bullets, use the drop-down arrow beside the bullets icon 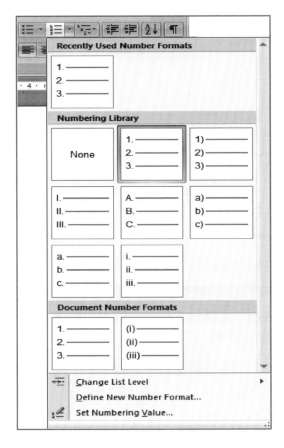 and click on the number format you want.

To remove numbering, select the text from which you want to remove the numbering, click on the numbering icon on the toolbar and the numbering is removed.

Text Alignment

Right Align

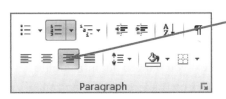

To right align the text, first highlight the text you want to right align and click on the right alignment icon on the Paragraph section under the HOME tab.

Left Align

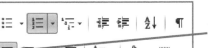

To left align the text, first highlight the text you want to left align and click on the left alignment icon on the Paragraph section under the HOME tab.

Centre Align

To centre text, first highlight the text you want to centre and click on the centre alignment icon on the Paragraph section under the HOME tab.

Justify

To justify text, first highlight the text you want to justify and click on the justify icon on the Paragraph section under the HOME tab.

Line Spacing

Select the Line Spacing icon on the Paragraph section under the HOME tab.

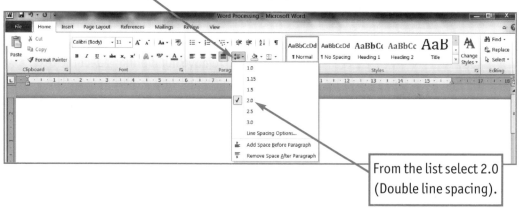

From the list select 2.0 (Double line spacing).

OR

Highlight the text you want to put into double line spacing. Click on the arrow at the bottom of the Paragraph section under the HOME tab.

Under Line Spacing change to Double and click OK.

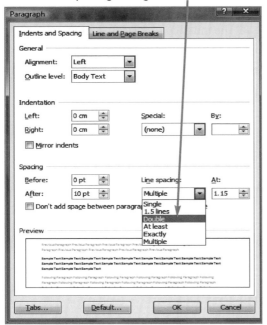

Indentation

Highlight the area that you need to indent, then click and drag the left margin indent (click on square part on the bottom) and pull it in on the ruler line.

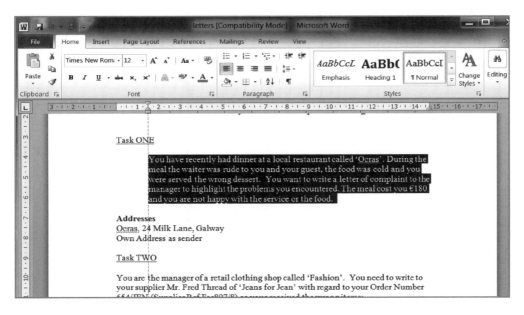

OR

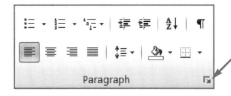

To set the indent distance on your margin, click on the arrow at the bottom of the Paragraph section under the HOME tab.

Then select the size or distance you want for your indentation using the arrows. Then click OK.

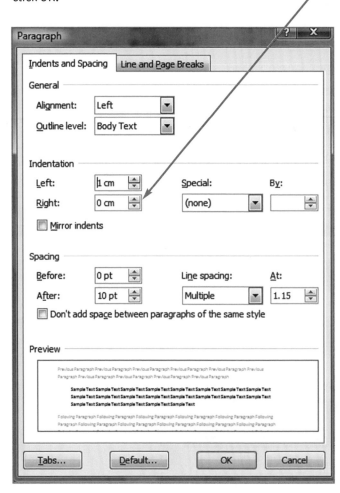

THE BASIC GUIDE TO WORD PROCESSING

Indenting the Right Margin

Highlight the area that you need to indent, then click and drag the right margin indent (click on bottom arrow) and pull it in the distance you require on the ruler line.

Paragraph Spacing

To set the space between paragraphs, click on the arrow at the bottom of the Paragraph section under the HOME tab.

Select the spacing you want **before** or **after** the paragraph.

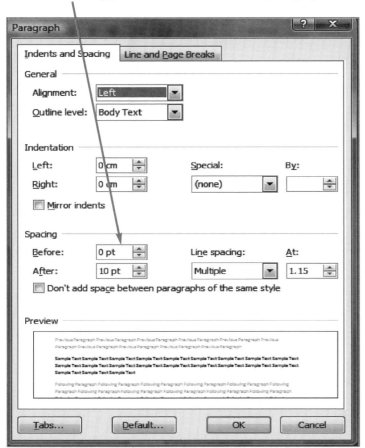

Setting Tabs and Tab Leaders

To set tabs in your document, click on the arrow at the bottom of the Paragraph section under the HOME tab.

Select the Tabs button at the end of the Paragraph window.

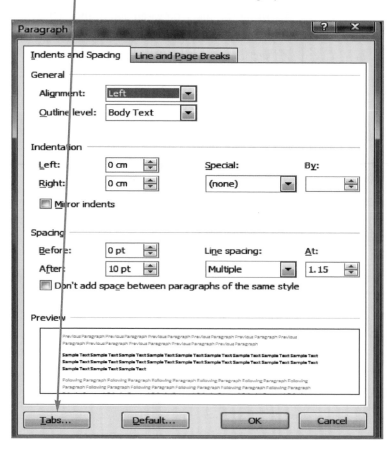

THE BASIC GUIDE TO WORD PROCESSING

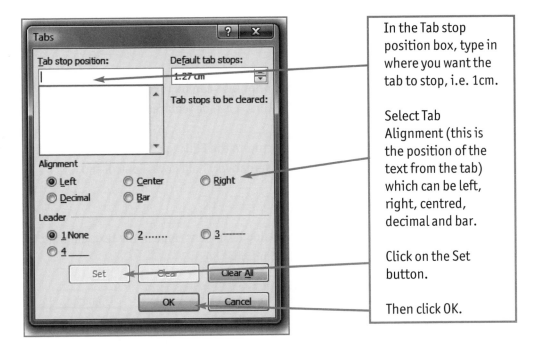

In the Tab stop position box, type in where you want the tab to stop, i.e. 1cm.

Select Tab Alignment (this is the position of the text from the tab) which can be left, right, centred, decimal and bar.

Click on the Set button.

Then click OK.

New tab positions are calculated by counting the number of spaces in the longest word(s) in each column. Allow for spaces between the columns.

Note: Clearing tabs: Select Clear All to clear all existing tabs and click OK. Select Clear to clear only one tab and click OK.

Tab Leaders

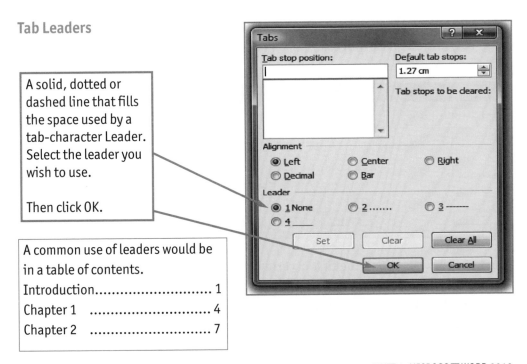

A solid, dotted or dashed line that fills the space used by a tab-character Leader. Select the leader you wish to use.

Then click OK.

A common use of leaders would be in a table of contents.

Introduction............................ 1

Chapter 1   4

Chapter 2   7

Find and Replace

One or every occurrence of a specific word or phrase can be found and replaced in MS Word, e.g. wherever the word "computer" occurs, it can be replaced with "PC".

 Select the Find drop-down arrow in the Editing section of the HOME Tab and select Advanced Find. (Alternatively hold down Control and F.)

When the Find and Replace dialog box opens, type in the text you want to find (e.g. "Computer" in the Find what box).

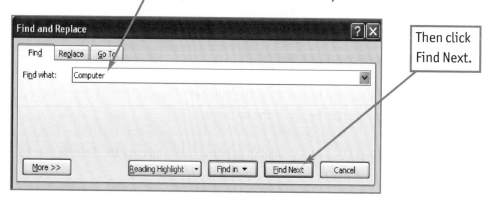

Then click Find Next.

Click on the REPLACE tab and type the word you want to replace your original word with (e.g. "PC") in the Replace with box.

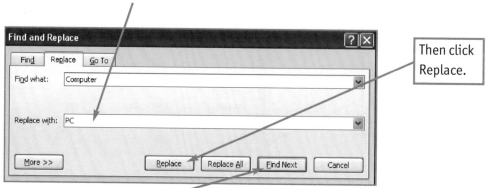

Then click Replace.

When you click Find Next, the first occurrence of "computer" is highlighted, click on Replace to replace one occurrence of the word. To replace all occurrences of the word, click on Replace All, so it is changed wherever it appears in the text.

Note: Clicking Find Next twice in succession allows you to skip an occurrence of the word without replacing it.

Find

If you want to find text (without using Find and Replace), you can click Find.

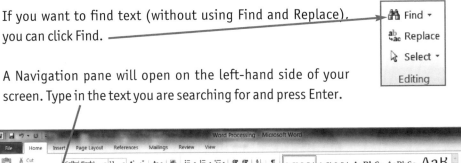

A Navigation pane will open on the left-hand side of your screen. Type in the text you are searching for and press Enter.

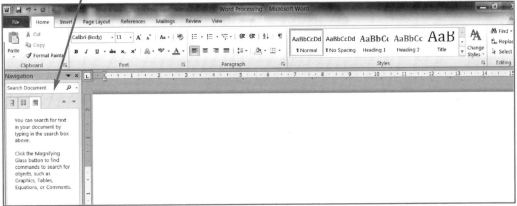

Example:

I am looking for the word "paste".

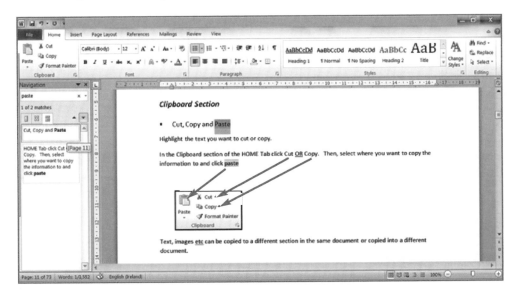

3. INSERT TAB

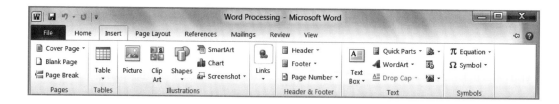

Tables Section
Setting up Tables

Click on the Table section under the INSERT tab.

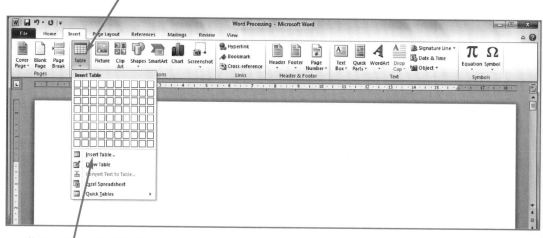

Click on Insert Table, then choose the number of rows and columns you wish to have in the table.

Once you have selected the number of rows and columns you need, click OK.

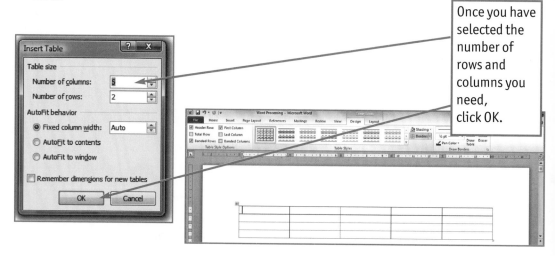

Changing Column Width in a Table

Rest the mouse I-beam on the column divider. The I-beam changes to a left/right arrow shape. Then click and hold this shape.

Drag the left/right arrow to the left to reduce the column width and to the right to widen the column width.

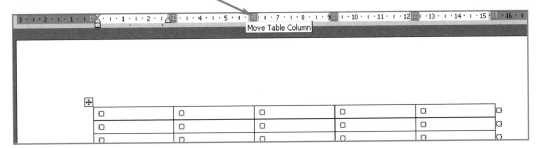

Inserting Rows in a Table

When you insert a table, the TABLE TOOLS tabs appear on your Menu bar. One tab relates to the **design** of your table and the other relates to the **layout** of your table.

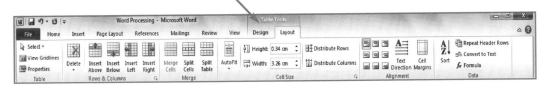

To insert rows in your table, position the cursor in the correct place for inserting rows above or rows below the cursor. Select the LAYOUT tab.

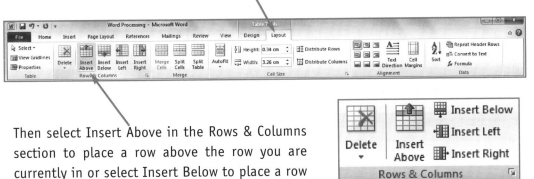

Then select Insert Above in the Rows & Columns section to place a row above the row you are currently in or select Insert Below to place a row below the row you are currently in.

OR

Position the cursor in the correct place for inserting rows above or rows below the cursor. Right click on the mouse and select Insert. Then select Insert Rows Above or Rows Below.

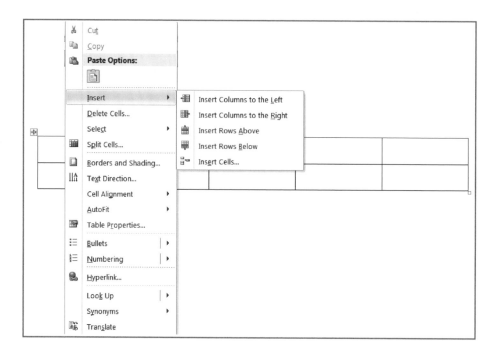

Inserting Columns in a Table

When you insert a table, TABLE TOOLS tabs appear on your Menu bar. One tab relates to the **design** of your table and the other relates to the **layout** of your table.

To insert a column in your table select the LAYOUT tab.

Position the cursor in the correct place for inserting columns to the left or right of the cursor.

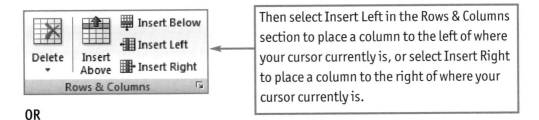

Then select Insert Left in the Rows & Columns section to place a column to the left of where your cursor currently is, or select Insert Right to place a column to the right of where your cursor currently is.

OR

Position the cursor in the correct place for inserting a column to the left or right of the cursor. Right click on the mouse and select Insert. Then select Insert Column to the Left or Insert Column to the Right.

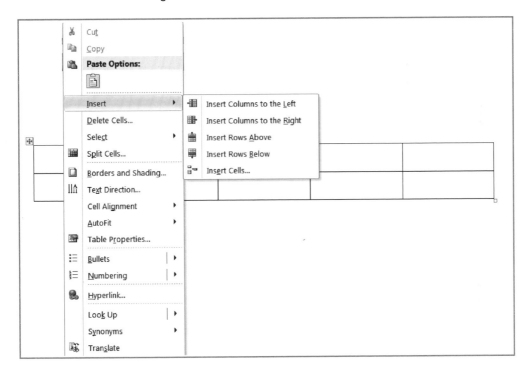

Deleting Rows or Columns in Tables

Highlight the rows (or columns) that you want to delete in the table. Select Delete in the Rows & Columns section (in the TABLE TOOLS Layout tab).

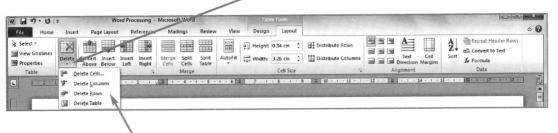

Select Delete Rows (or Delete Columns).

Changing Border Thickness in Tables

When you insert a table, the TABLE TOOLS tabs appear on your Menu bar. One tab relates to the **design** of your table and the other relates to the **layout** of your table.

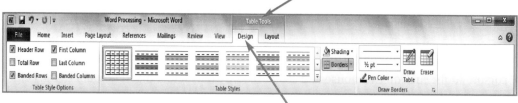

To change border thickness in tables, select the DESIGN tab.

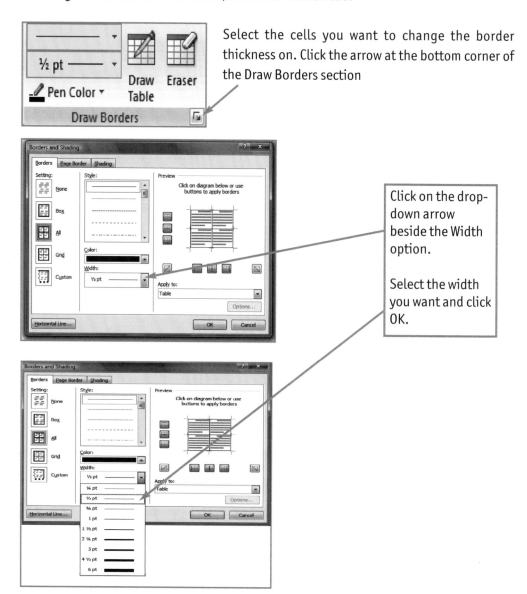

Select the cells you want to change the border thickness on. Click the arrow at the bottom corner of the Draw Borders section

Click on the drop-down arrow beside the Width option.

Select the width you want and click OK.

Making Data Bold and Alignment in Tables

Highlight the text you want to edit and select the bold icon/alignment icons.

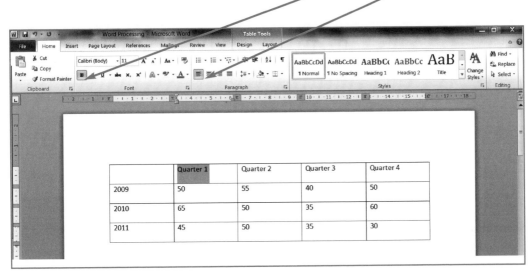

Shading in Column Headings

Highlight the cells you want to shade. In the Table Styles section of the TABLE TOOLS Design tab, select the drop-down arrow beside Shading.

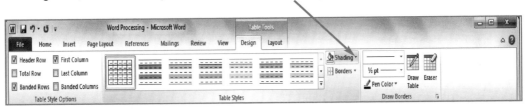

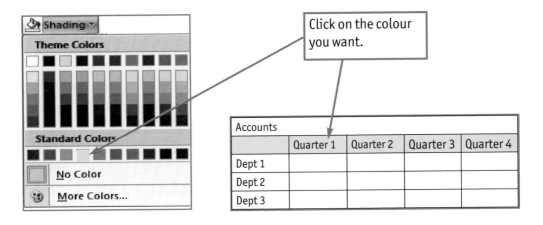

Click on the colour you want.

Merging Cells in a Table

Highlight the cells you want to merge. In the Merge Section of the TABLE TOOLS Layout tab, select Merge Cells.

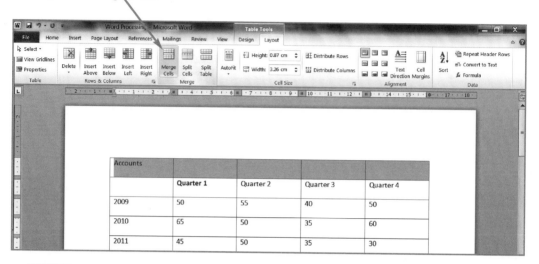

Merged cells

Sorting Data in a Table

Highlight the cells that you need to sort. Select Sort in the Data section of the TABLE TOOLS Layout tab.

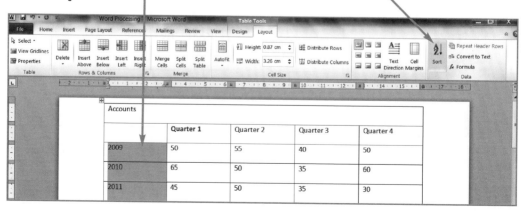

The following options menu will appear. Select the Column you want to sort by,

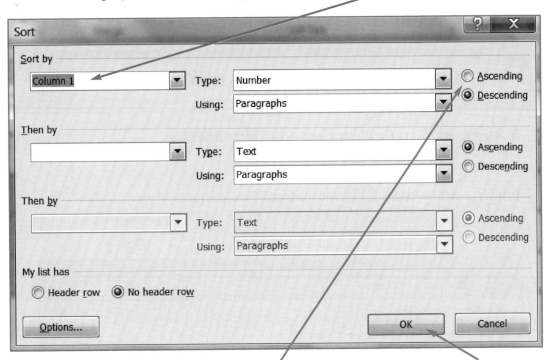

then the Type and whether you want it in Ascending or Descending order. Then click OK.

Your table will now be sorted.

Accounts				
	Quarter 1	Quarter 2	Quarter 3	Quarter 4
2011	45	50	35	30
2010	65	50	35	60
2009	50	55	40	50

Illustrations Section

Graphics

To insert graphics, use the Illustrations section of the INSERT tab.

To insert a picture, select [Picture] and the Insert Picture screen will open.

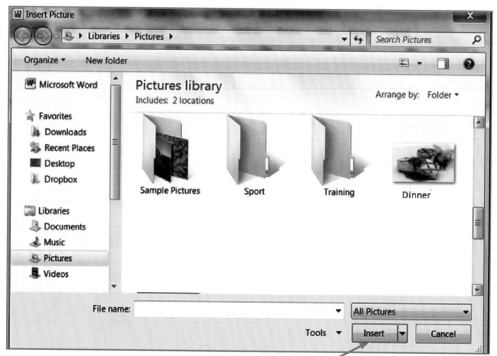

Select the picture you wish to use and click Insert.

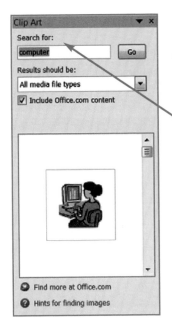

To insert a clip art image, select 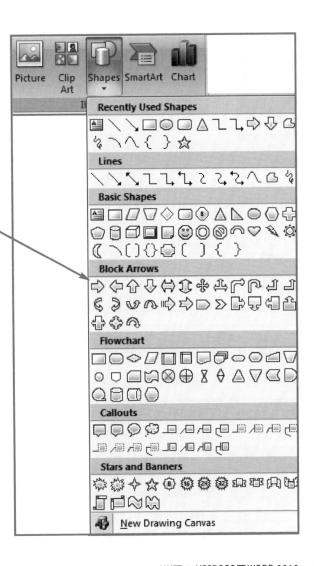 and the clip art panel will open on the right-hand side of your screen.

In the Search for box type in what you want to find a clip art picture of and click Go.

To insert a Shape, select and the Shapes screen will open. Click on the shape you want to use.

Manipulating Graphics, e.g. Borders, Resizing

To manipulate any graphic click on the graphic and a new Picture Tools toolbar will appear above your Menu bar. This opens a FORMAT tab that you can then use to manipulate the graphic.

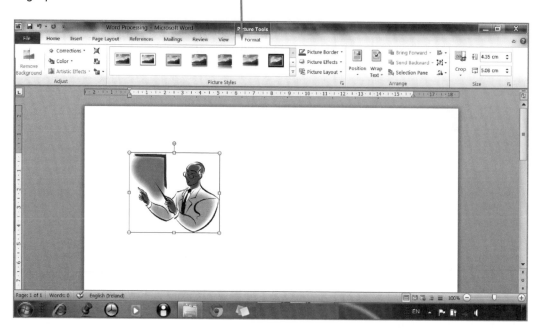

The FORMAT tab allows you to manipulate the graphic in a number of ways.

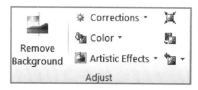

Adjust

Picture Styles (including Borders)

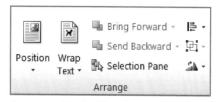

Arrange (including Text Wrapping)

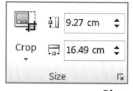

Size

Header and Footer Section
Headers and Footers

Header

In this toolbar you will find all the tools available for use in your header and footers. Click on the INSERT tab at the top of the Menu bar.

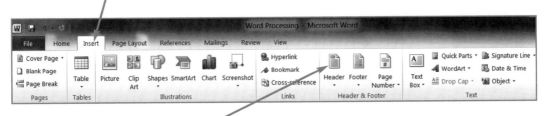

To insert a header, click on Header on the Header & Footer section.

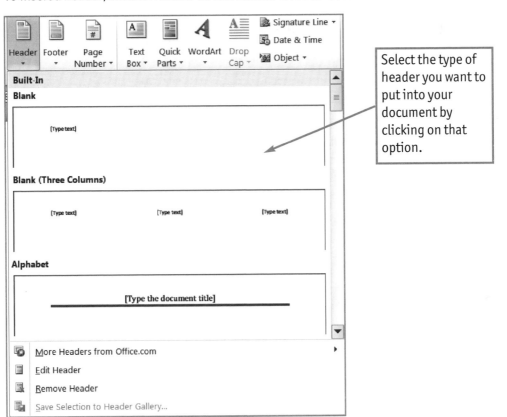

Select the type of header you want to put into your document by clicking on that option.

Once you select the type of header you want, it is inserted into your document and a new toolbar opens – Header & Footer Tools, Design.

In this toolbar you will find all the tools available for use in your header and footers.

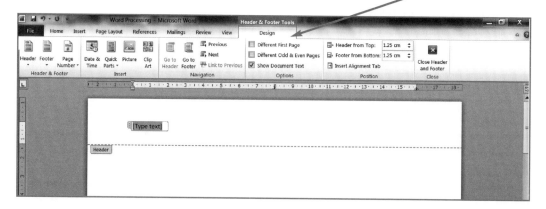

Footer

Click on the INSERT tab at the top of the Menu bar.

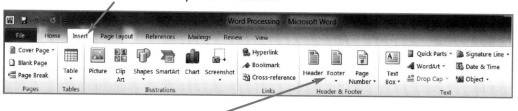

To insert a footer, click on Footer on the Header & Footer section.

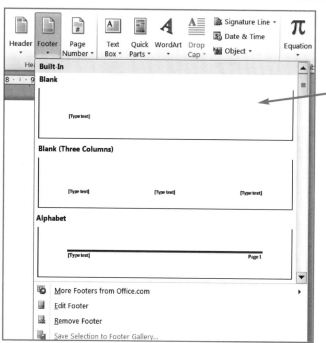

Select the type of header you want to put into your document by clicking on that option.

Once you select the type of footer you want it is inserted into your document and a new toolbar opens.

In this toolbar you will find all the tools available for use in your header and footers.

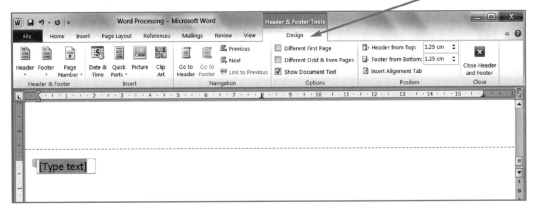

Page Numbering

Click on the INSERT tab at the top of the Menu bar.

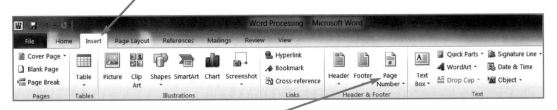

To insert page numbers, click on Page Number on the Header & Footer section.

A drop-down menu of options will appear.

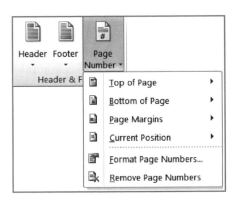

Select where you want the page numbers (i.e. top of page, bottom of page etc) and how you want to position them (i.e. left, centre, right etc.).

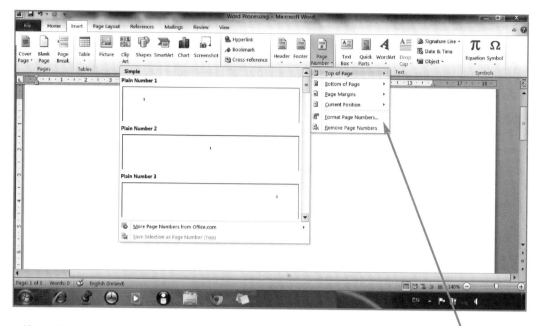

Note: You can also change the format of the page numbers by selecting Format Page Numbers on the drop-down menu.

Symbols Section

International and Special Characters

In the Symbols section under the INSERT tab click on Symbol.

Click on the symbol you want to use.
Then click Insert.

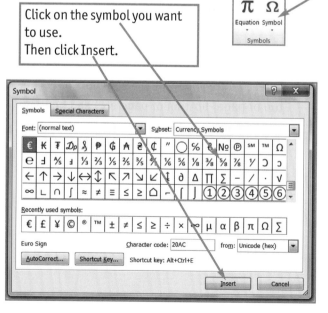

If the symbol or special character you need is not in the commonly used symbols that appear, click on More Symbols. This will give an extensive collection of symbols to choose from.

THE BASIC GUIDE TO WORD PROCESSING

4. PAGE LAYOUT

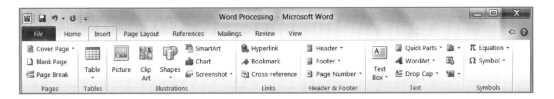

Page Setup Section

Indentation

1. To indent a whole block of selected text by 2 cm.
2. Select the text you want to indent.
3. In the Paragraph section of the PAGE LAYOUT tab

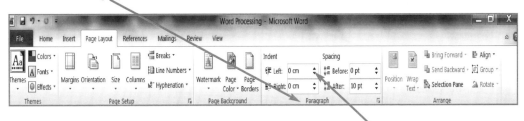

change the Indent setting using the arrow keys beside Left Indent.

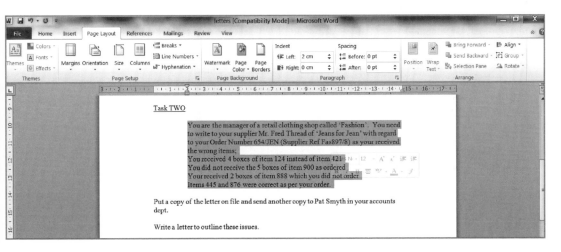

The selected text now starts 2 cm from the left-hand margin. (To indent from the right as well, increase the setting to 2 cm, using the arrow keys of the Right Indent).

OR

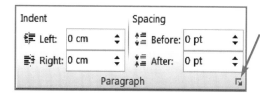

Select the arrow at the bottom corner of the Paragraph section of the PAGE LAYOUT (or HOME) tab.

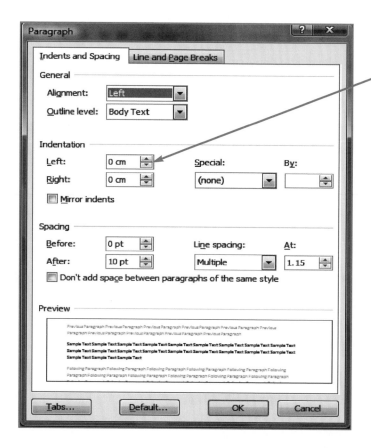

Change the setting using the arrow keys beside Left indent (or Right).

Page, Section and Column Breaks

Inserting Page, Column and Section Breaks

In the Page setup section under the PAGE LAYOUT Tab click on Breaks.

A drop-down list of Break options will appear, click on the type of Break you want to use in your document.

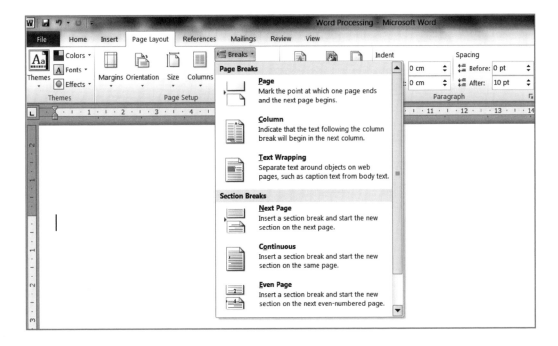

Columns

Producing Text in Multiple Columns

In the Page setup section under the PAGE LAYOUT tab click on Columns.

A drop-down list of Column options will appear. Click on the number of columns you want to use in your document.

If you want to select a specific layout for your columns, click on More Columns and an additional menu will appear.

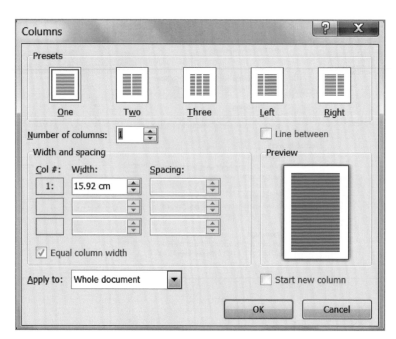

THE BASIC GUIDE TO WORD PROCESSING

5. MAILING

Start Mail Merge Section

Mail Merge and Labels

In the MAILING tab select Start Mail Merge in the Start Mail Merge section.

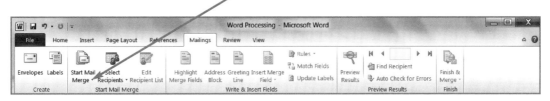

In the drop-down menu select Step by Step Mail Merge Wizard.

A Mail Merge Wizard will open on the right of your screen.

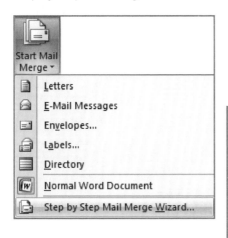

1. Select the type of document you want to create.
2. Click on Next: Starting Document.

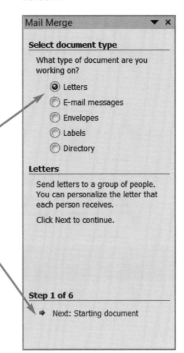

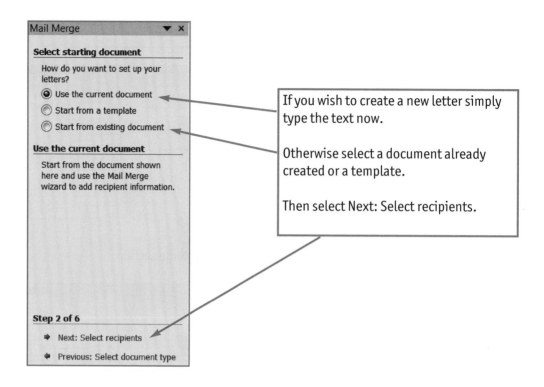

Mail Merge

Select starting document

How do you want to set up your letters?

◉ Use the current document

◯ Start from a template

◯ Start from existing document

Use the current document

Start from the document shown here and use the Mail Merge wizard to add recipient information.

Step 2 of 6

➡ Next: Select recipients

⬅ Previous: Select document type

If you wish to create a new letter simply type the text now.

Otherwise select a document already created or a template.

Then select Next: Select recipients.

Example

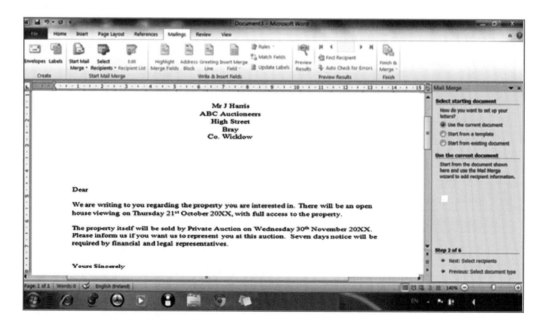

There are two options available to you:

1. You can choose the recipients of the mail merge letter from a database or spreadsheet you have already created.

2. You can create a data source of recipients if you do not have one already.

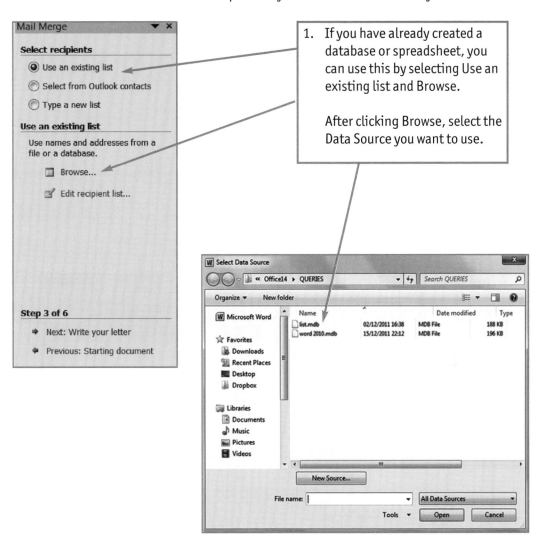

1. If you have already created a database or spreadsheet, you can use this by selecting Use an existing list and Browse.

   After clicking Browse, select the Data Source you want to use.

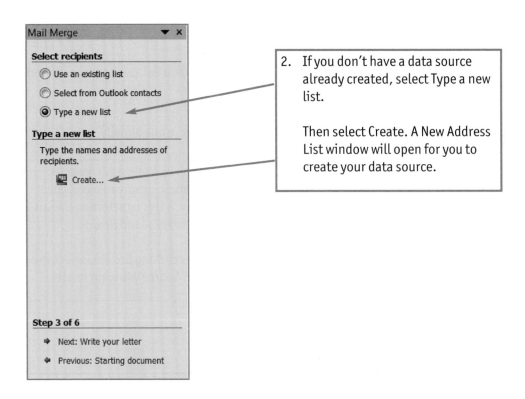

Mail Merge ▼ ✕

Select recipients

◯ Use an existing list

◯ Select from Outlook contacts

◉ Type a new list

Type a new list

Type the names and addresses of recipients.

🖳 Create...

Step 3 of 6

➡ Next: Write your letter

⬅ Previous: Starting document

2. If you don't have a data source already created, select Type a new list.

Then select Create. A New Address List window will open for you to create your data source.

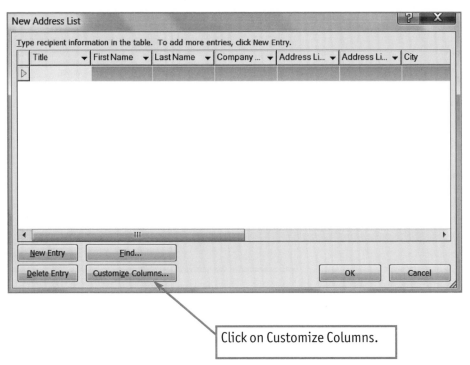

New Address List

Type recipient information in the table. To add more entries, click New Entry.

	Title ▼	First Name ▼	Last Name ▼	Company ... ▼	Address Li... ▼	Address Li... ▼	City
▷							

New Entry   Find...

Delete Entry   Customize Columns...   OK   Cancel

Click on Customize Columns.

Delete the fields you do not need and add any fields you require. Then click OK.

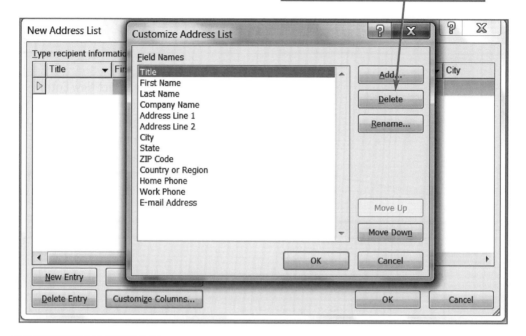

Add the information for the people you wish to receive the letter.

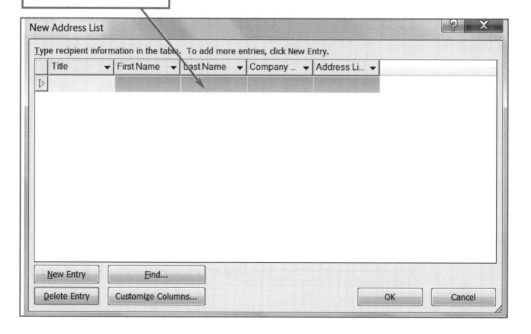

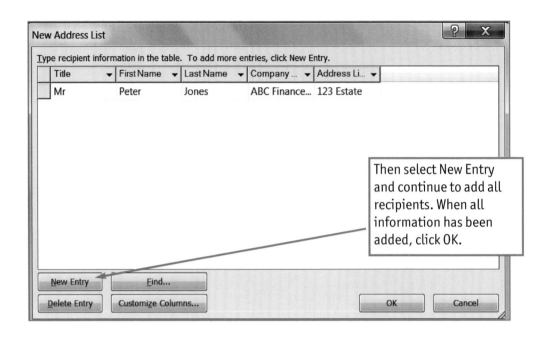

Then select New Entry and continue to add all recipients. When all information has been added, click OK.

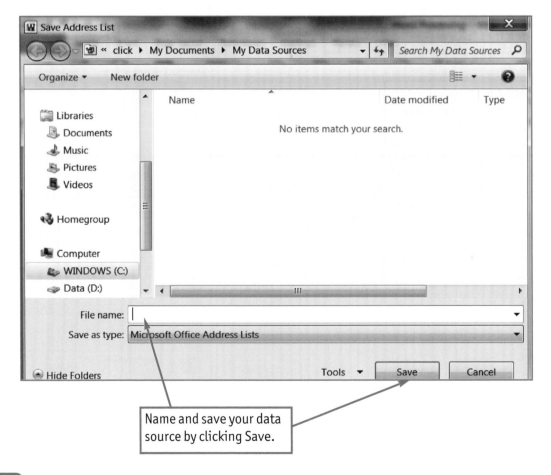

Name and save your data source by clicking Save.

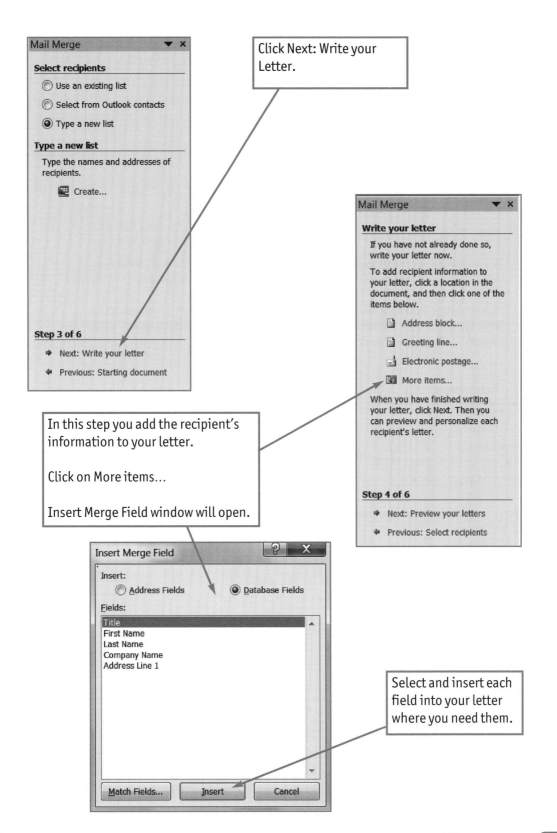

Mail Merge ▼ ✕

Select recipients

- ⦾ Use an existing list
- ⦾ Select from Outlook contacts
- ⦿ Type a new list

Type a new list

Type the names and addresses of recipients.

🖼 Create...

Step 3 of 6

➡ Next: Write your letter

⬅ Previous: Starting document

Click Next: Write your Letter.

Mail Merge ▼ ✕

Write your letter

If you have not already done so, write your letter now.

To add recipient information to your letter, click a location in the document, and then click one of the items below.

- 📄 Address block...
- 📄 Greeting line...
- 🖃 Electronic postage...
- 🖼 More items...

When you have finished writing your letter, click Next. Then you can preview and personalize each recipient's letter.

Step 4 of 6

➡ Next: Preview your letters

⬅ Previous: Select recipients

In this step you add the recipient's information to your letter.

Click on More items...

Insert Merge Field window will open.

Insert Merge Field ❓ ✕

Insert:
- ⦾ Address Fields ⦿ Database Fields

Fields:

Title
First Name
Last Name
Company Name
Address Line 1

Select and insert each field into your letter where you need them.

Match Fields... | Insert | Cancel

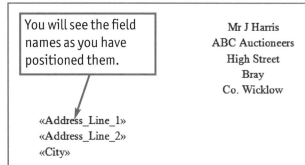
Mr J Harris
ABC Auctioneers
High Street
Bray
Co. Wicklow

«Address_Line_1»
«Address_Line_2»
«City»

Dear «Title» «First_Name» «Last_Name»

We are writing to you regarding the property you are interested in. There will be an open house viewing on Thursday 21st October 20XX, with full access to the property.

The property itself will be sold by Private Auction on Wednesday 30th November 20XX. Please inform us if you want us to represent you at this auction. Seven days notice will be required by financial and legal representatives.

Yours Sincerely

Step 4 of 6

➡ Next: Preview your letters
⬅ Previous: Select recipients

Then click on Preview your letters.

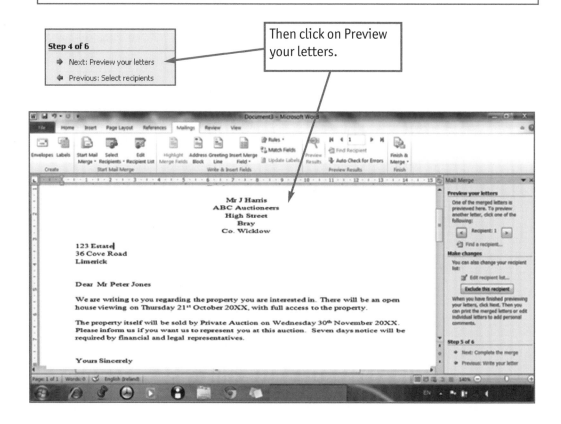

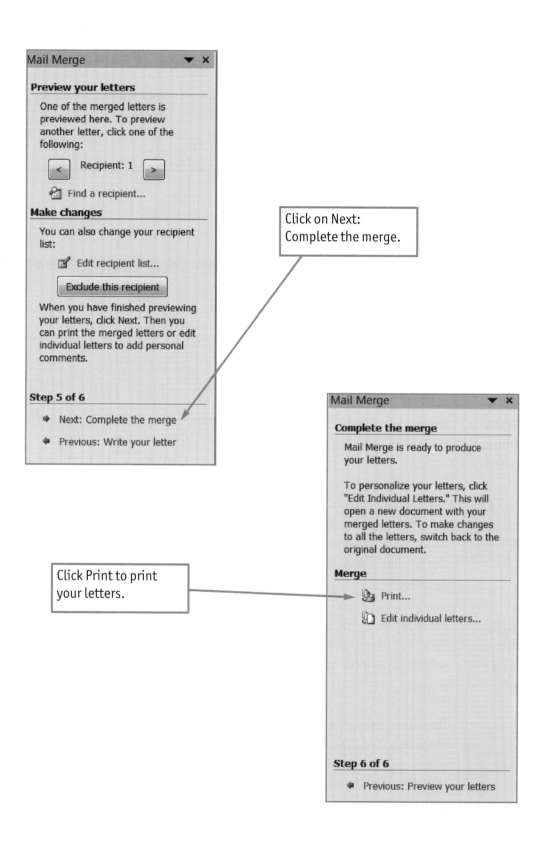

Mail Merge ▼ ✕

Preview your letters

One of the merged letters is previewed here. To preview another letter, click one of the following:

| < | Recipient: 1 | > |

📇 Find a recipient...

Make changes

You can also change your recipient list:

✏️ Edit recipient list...

Exclude this recipient

When you have finished previewing your letters, click Next. Then you can print the merged letters or edit individual letters to add personal comments.

Step 5 of 6

➡ Next: Complete the merge

⬅ Previous: Write your letter

Click on Next: Complete the merge.

Mail Merge ▼ ✕

Complete the merge

Mail Merge is ready to produce your letters.

To personalize your letters, click "Edit Individual Letters." This will open a new document with your merged letters. To make changes to all the letters, switch back to the original document.

Merge

🖨 Print...

📑 Edit individual letters...

Click Print to print your letters.

Step 6 of 6

⬅ Previous: Preview your letters

6. REVIEW

Proofing Section
Proofing Tools

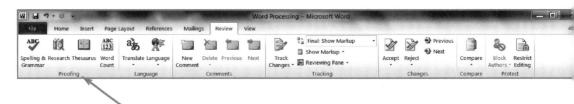

In the proofing section under the REVIEW tab there are a number of proofing tools: Spelling and Grammar, Research, Thesaurus, Translate, Translation Tip Screen, Set Language and Word Count.

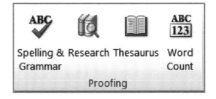

 Spelling & Grammar: This allows you to check your document for spelling and grammar mistakes. Lines appear under words or sentences in your document which are spelt incorrectly or where incorrect grammar has been used. Select the Spelling & Grammar icon to go through the document and correct these mistakes.

 Research: When you select this icon, the Research pane opens on the right-hand side of your screen. It allows you to look up a variety of research and reference services such as dictionaries, encyclopedias and translation services.

 Thesaurus: Select the word you want to use in the thesaurus, then select the Thesaurus icon. The Research pane opens on the right-hand side of your screen giving a list of suggestions of other words with a similar meaning to the word you selected in your text. You can then replace your original word with one of these suggestions, if preferred.

Translate: This allows you to translate your text into a different language.

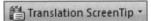

Translation ScreenTip: When you select this icon, you can turn on the ScreenTip. When you pause your cursor on a word, a text box appears over the word giving you the translation of that word in your chosen language.

Set Language: Select the language you want to use to check the spelling and grammar in your document.

Word Count: When you select Word Count, a text box appears on your screen telling you the number of Words, Characters, Paragraphs and Lines in your document. Word Count can also be seen on the status bar at the bottom of your page.

7. VIEW

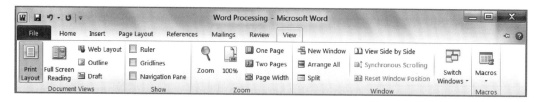

Document Views Section

Screen Views

To change the screen view (this only changes the way the document looks on the computer screen) simply click on the screen view options in the Document View Section of the VIEW tab.

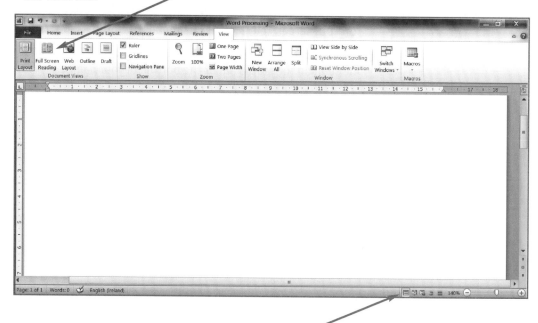

Or click on the screen view options on the bottom right-hand side of your screen.

The options available are:

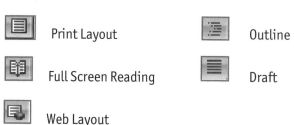

Print Layout		Outline	
Full Screen Reading		Draft	
Web Layout			

There is also the option to view the screen at different sizes by changing the zoom from 10% to 500%.

Show/Hide Section

Ruler

To show the ruler on your screen, go to the VIEW Tab and tick the Ruler box in the Show/Hide section.

8. FILE MANAGEMENT

Folders and Subfolders

Setting up a Folder or a Subfolder on a Drive

Make sure the USB key is in the drive.
Select the Start icon, then Computer, then USB key (removable disk).

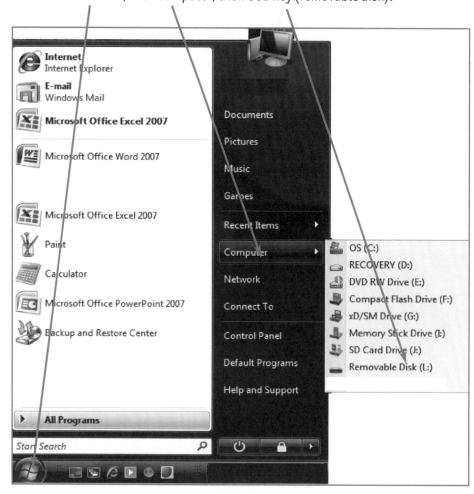

Select File, select New, Select Folder. (Alternatively place the cursor in
panel and right click on the mouse to

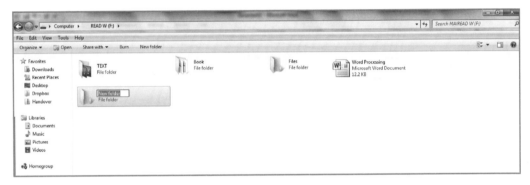

Then name the new folder by simply typing in the highlighted box.

To set up subfolders
on a drive, click on the
new folder that has
been made and repeat
what you have just
done to create a new
folder (i.e. a folder
inside another folder
is known as a
subfolder). Name the
new subfolder.

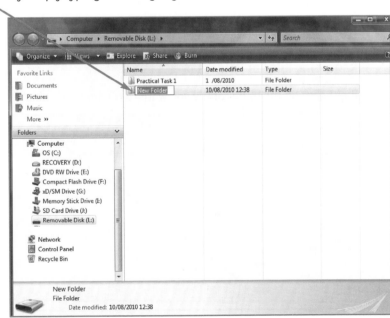

opying and Renaming Files and Folders

Copying a File or Folder

Select the file or folder you want to copy, then select Organize and select Copy.

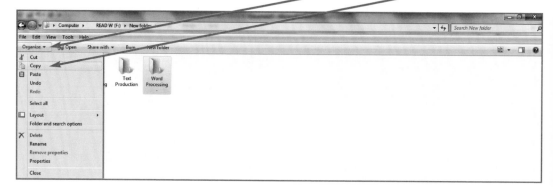

Select where you want to copy the file or folder, then select Organize and select Paste.

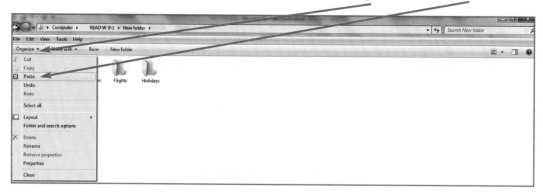

Note: You can also move files and folders by selecting the Move To icon on the toolbar.

Renaming Files or Folders

Right click on the folder or file you want to rename and select Rename.

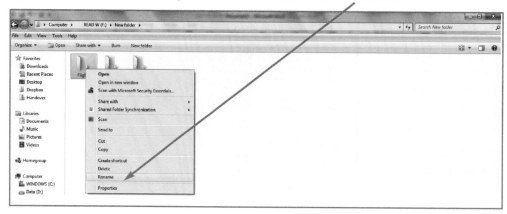

THE BASIC GUIDE TO WORD PROCESSING

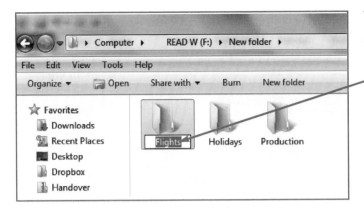

Then name the new folder by simply typing in the highlighted box.

File Information

Click on the Start Icon, then select Computer and select where your file is stored.

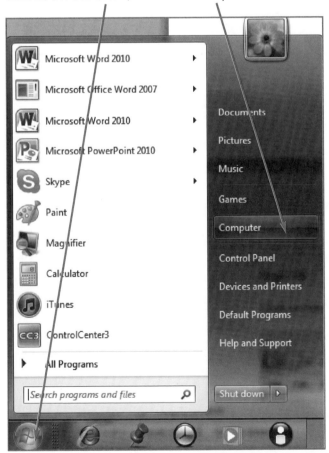

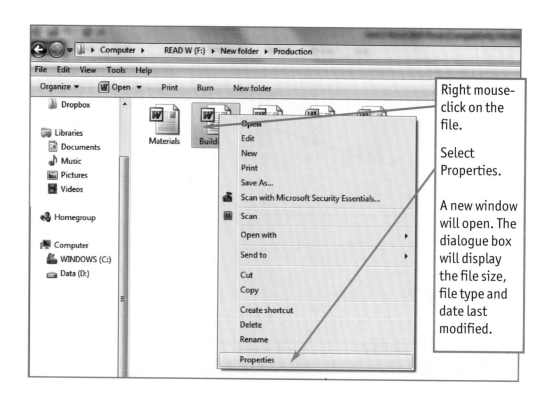

Right mouse-click on the file.

Select Properties.

A new window will open. The dialogue box will display the file size, file type and date last modified.

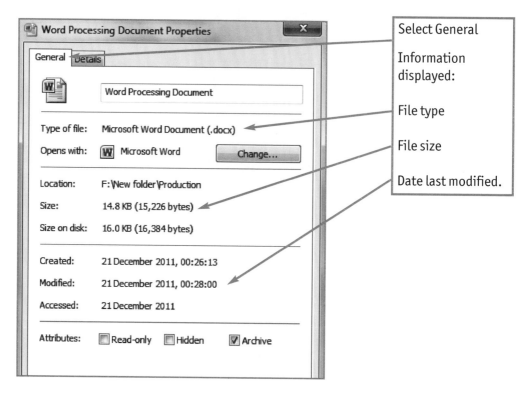

Select General

Information displayed:

File type

File size

Date last modified.

Search Facility

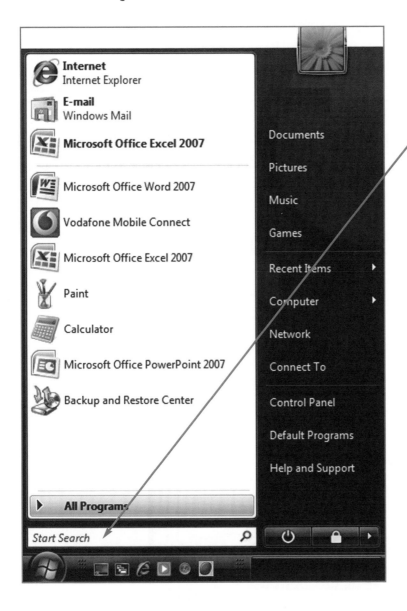

To search, select the Start icon and type what you are searching for into the Search box.

Using the Help Facility

The help facility in MS Word 2010 is located on the top left-hand side of the screen.

Click on the blue and white question mark and the Help menu will appear.

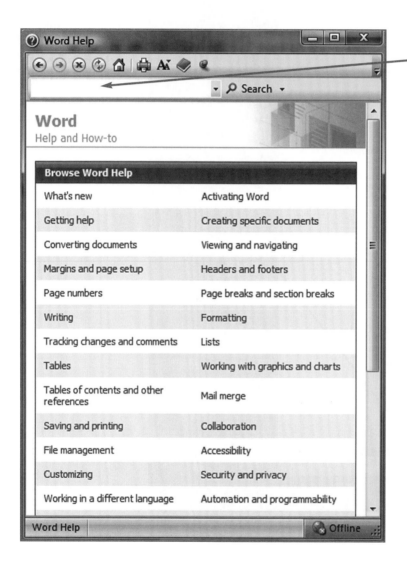

Simply type what you want help with into the Search box and click Search.

OFFICE BUTTON AND QUICK ACCESS TOOLBAR

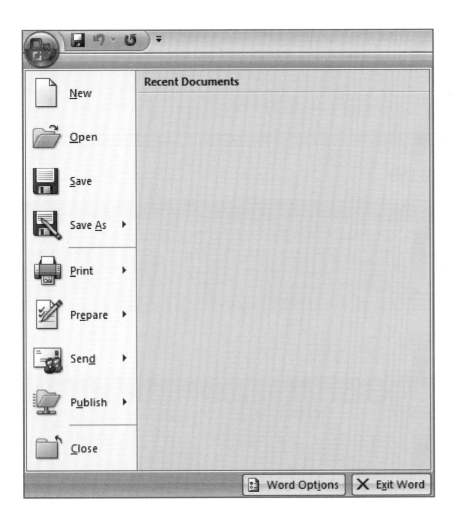

HOME TAB

INSERT TAB

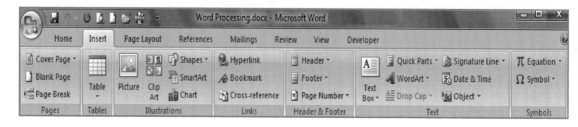

PAGE LAYOUT TAB

REFERENCES TAB

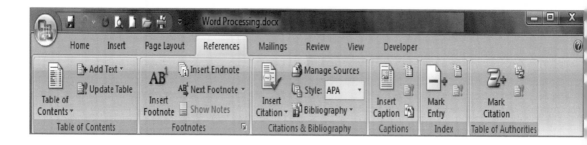

MAILINGS TAB

REVIEW TAB

VIEW TAB

DEVELOPER TAB

1. OFFICE BUTTON

Creating a Document

To create a new document click on the Office button and select New.

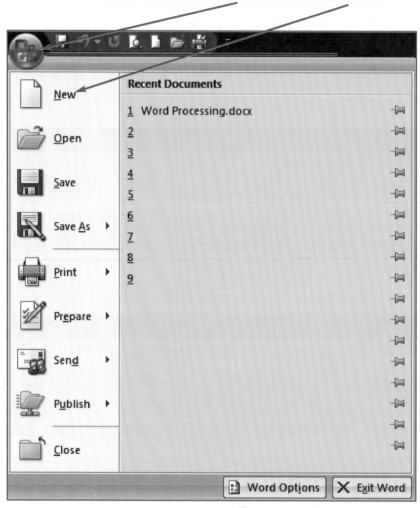

Templates

To create and apply a template, click on the Microsoft Office Button and select New.

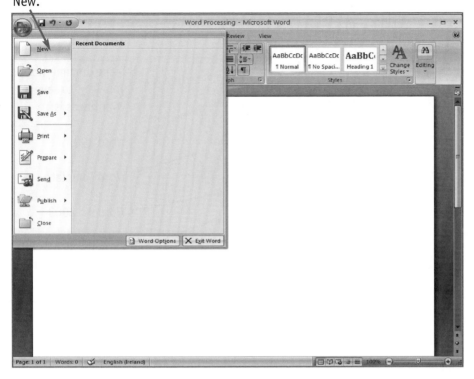

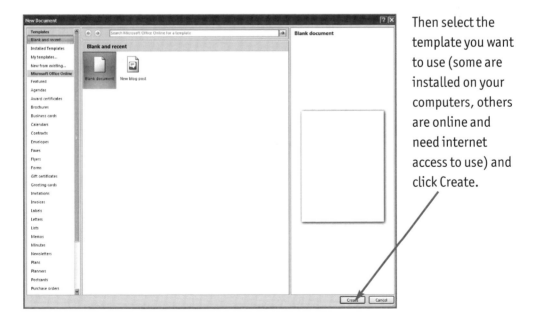

Then select the template you want to use (some are installed on your computers, others are online and need internet access to use) and click Create.

Save As

Save documents as: Document, Text File, web page etc.

1. To save your document, click on the Microsoft Office Button 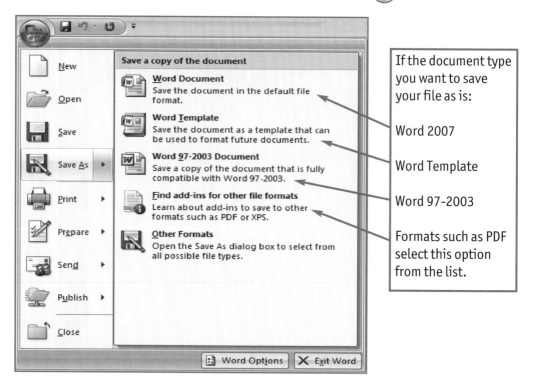 and select Save as.

If the document type you want to save your file as is:

Word 2007

Word Template

Word 97-2003

Formats such as PDF select this option from the list.

2. If you want to save your document as a text file, web page etc, select the Other Formats option.

In the Save as type section, use the drop arrow to select the type of file you want to save your document as and click Save.

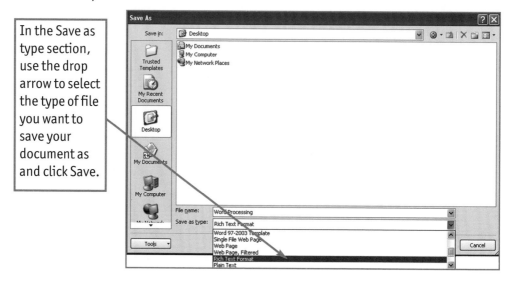

Print

You can use a range of print features, e.g. print, preview, print single/multiple copies, print specific pages.

To print your document click on the Microsoft Office button and select Print.

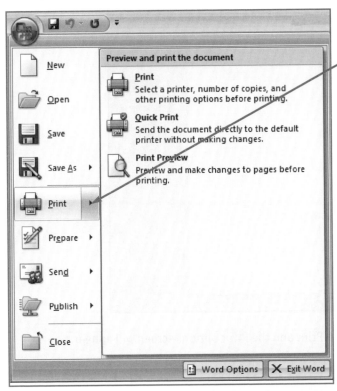

To preview your documents before printing them, use the Print Preview option.

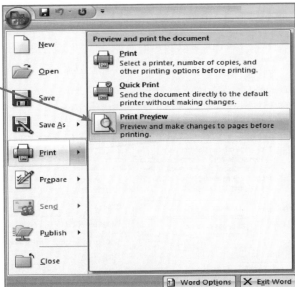

The Preview window opens, view your document and close by clicking on Close Print Preview.

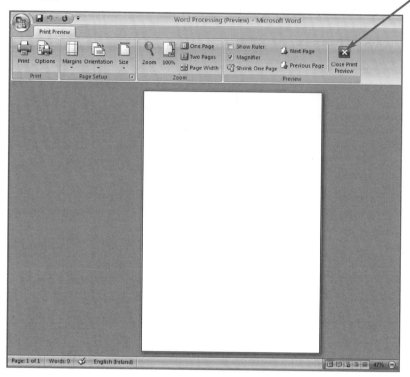

To print your document, click on Print and the Print options screen will appear.

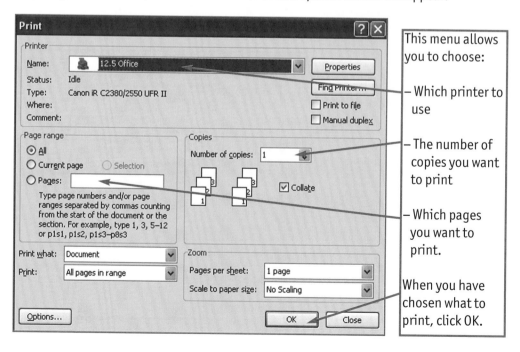

This menu allows you to choose:

– Which printer to use

– The number of copies you want to print

– Which pages you want to print.

When you have chosen what to print, click OK.

Properties such as colour or black and white printing, paper layout, paper size and quality of print can be changed by clicking on the Properties button.

2. HOME TAB

Clipboard Section

Cut, Copy and Paste

Highlight the text you want to cut or copy.
In the Clipboard section of the HOME tab click Cut or Copy.

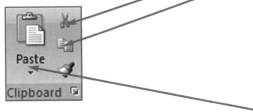

Then select where you want to copy the information to and click Paste.

Font Section

Making Text **Bold**, *Italic,* <u>Underlined</u> and Colour

Click on the HOME tab and highlight the text to format.

To make text **bold,** click **B** on the FORMATTING toolbar. **B**

To make text *italic,* click *I* on the FORMATTING toolbar. *I*

To <u>underline</u> text, click on the <u>Underline</u> icon on the FORMATTING toolbar. <u>**U**</u>

To underline text using different options, select the drop-down arrow.

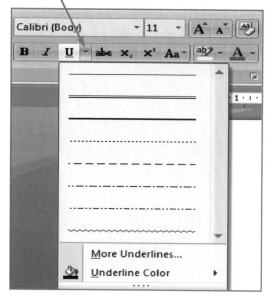

To put the text into colour, click on the  and use the drop-down arrow to select the colour.

Font Size

Click on the Font section of the HOME Tab. Highlight text for which you want to change the font size. Click on the font size icon on the FORMATTING toolbar and click on the drop-down arrow to select the number you want to set your font size.

OR

The font style, colour and size can all be chosen also by clicking on the arrow on the font bar and select Option needed in the Font window.

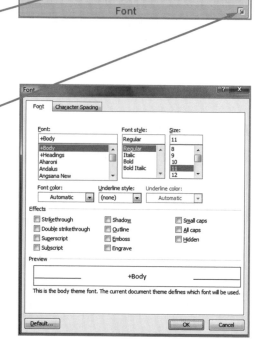

Font Effects

Highlight the text you want to use the effects on. Click on the arrow on the Font bar.

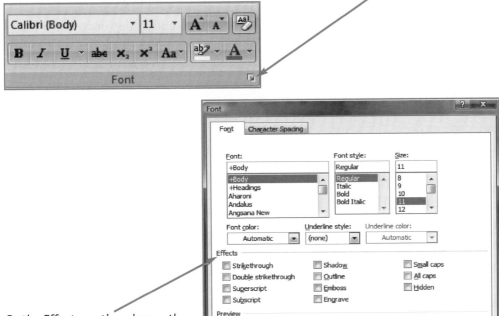

In the Effects section choose the effects you want to use on your text.

CAPITALS

Highlight the text to be put in capitals. Under the HOME tab click on **Aa▾** and select UPPERCASE.

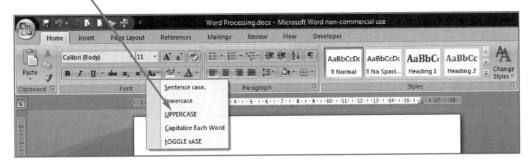

.

Note: This can also be used to change UPPERCASE to lowercase, to tOGGLE cASE and to Capitalize Each Word (Initial Capitals).

Paragraph Section
Bullets and Numbering

To add bullets to existing text, select the text to which you want to add bullets. Add bullets by clicking on the bullets icon ⊞▾ on the Paragraph section under the HOME tab.

To choose a different format for the bullets, use the drop-down arrow ⊞▾ beside the bullet icon and click on the bullet format you want.

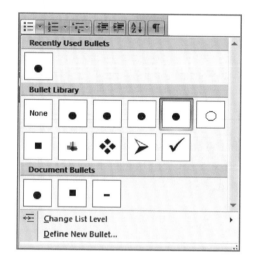

To remove bullets, select the text from which you want to remove bullets. Click on the bullets icon on the toolbar and the bullets are removed.

To add numbering, select the text to which you want to add numbering. Add numbering by clicking the numbers icon ⊞▾ on the Paragraph section under the HOME tab.

To choose a different format for the bullets, use the drop-down arrow beside the bullets icon 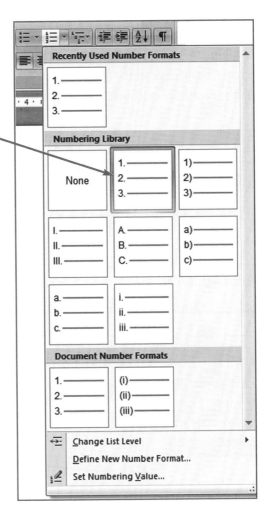 and click on the number format you want.

To remove numbering, select the text from which you want to remove numbering, click on the numbering icon on the toolbar and the numbering is removed.

Text Alignment

Right Align

To right align the text, first highlight the text you want to right align and click on the right alignment icon on the Paragraph section under the HOME tab.

Left Align

To left align the text, first highlight the text you want to left align and click on the left alignment icon on the Paragraph section under the HOME tab.

Centre Align

To centre text, first highlight the text you want to centre and click on the centre alignment icon on the Paragraph section under the HOME tab.

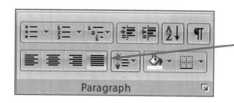

Justify

To justify the text, first highlight the text you want to justify and click on the justify icon on the Paragraph section under the HOME tab.

Line Spacing

Select the Line spacing icon 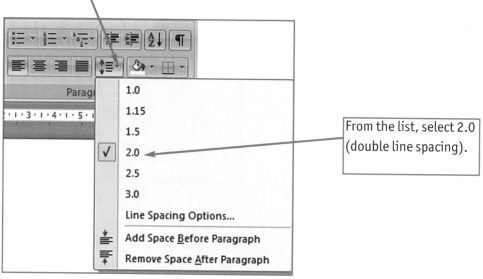 on the Paragraph section under the HOME tab.

From the list, select 2.0 (double line spacing).

OR

Highlight the text you want to put into double line spacing. Click on the arrow at the bottom of the Paragraph section under the HOME tab.

Under Line Spacing, change to Double and click OK.

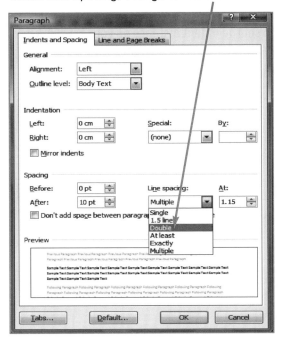

Indentation

Highlight the area that you need to indent, then click and drag the left margin indent (click on the square part at the bottom) and pull it in the distance you require on the ruler line.

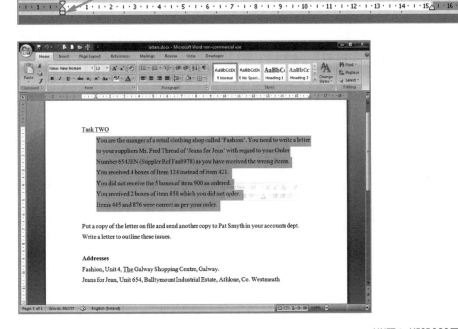

OR

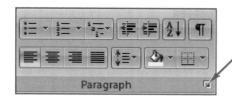

To set the indent distance on your margin, click on the arrow at the bottom of the Paragraph section under the HOME tab.

Use the arrows to select the size or distance you want for your indentation. Then click OK.

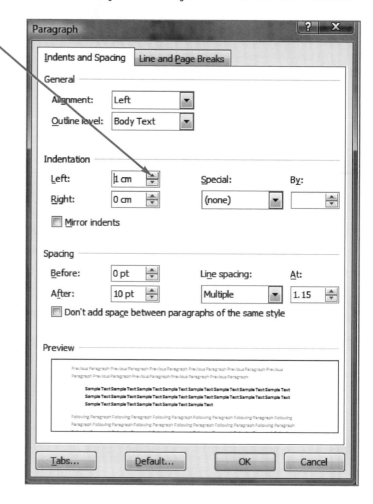

THE BASIC GUIDE TO WORD PROCESSING

Indenting the Right Margin

Highlight the area that you need to indent, then click and drag the right margin indent (click on the arrow at the bottom) and pull it in the distance you require on the ruler line.

Paragraph Spacing

To set the space between paragraphs, click on the arrow at the bottom of the Paragraph section under the HOME tab.

Select the spacing you want **before** or **after** the paragraph.

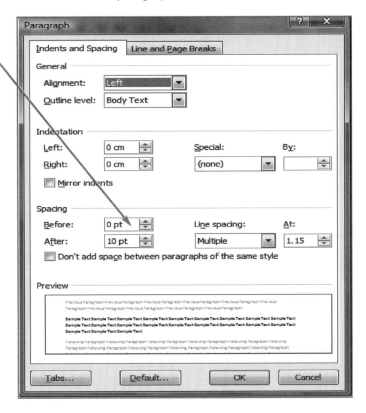

Setting Tabs and Tab Leaders

To set tabs in your document, click on the arrow at the bottom of the Paragraph section under the HOME tab.

Click on Tabs at the end of the Paragraph window.

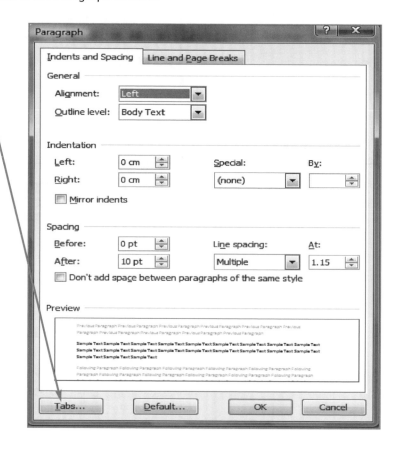

.

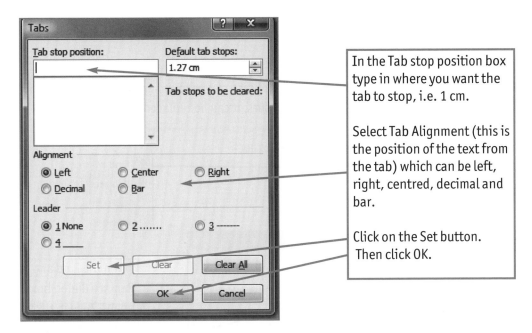

In the Tab stop position box type in where you want the tab to stop, i.e. 1 cm.

Select Tab Alignment (this is the position of the text from the tab) which can be left, right, centred, decimal and bar.

Click on the Set button. Then click OK.

Note: Clearing tabs: Select Clear All to clear all existing tabs and click OK. Select Clear to clear only one tab and click OK.

New tab positions are calculated by counting the number of spaces in the longest word(s) in each column. Allow for spaces between the columns.

Tab Leaders

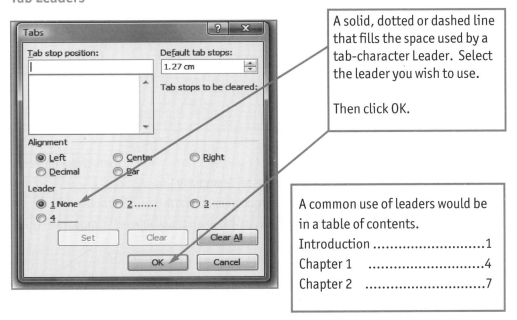

A solid, dotted or dashed line that fills the space used by a tab-character Leader. Select the leader you wish to use.

Then click OK.

A common use of leaders would be in a table of contents.

Introduction 1

Chapter 1 4

Chapter 2 7

Editing
Find and Replace

One or every occurrence of a specific word or phrase can be found and replaced in MS Word, e.g. wherever the word "computer" occurs, it can be replaced with "PC".

Select Find in the Editing section of the HOME tab (alternatively hold down Control and F).

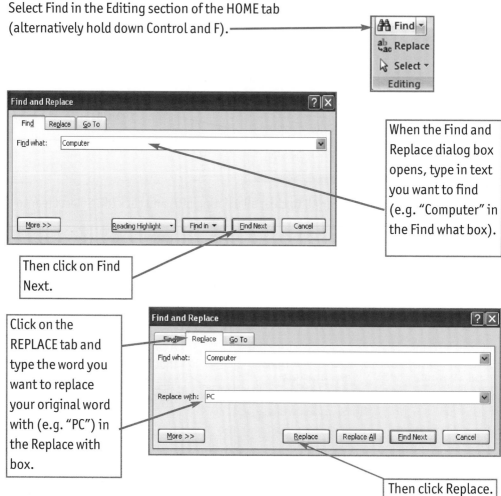

When the Find and Replace dialog box opens, type in text you want to find (e.g. "Computer" in the Find what box).

Then click on Find Next.

Click on the REPLACE tab and type the word you want to replace your original word with (e.g. "PC") in the Replace with box.

Then click Replace.

When you click Find Next, the first occurrence of "computer" is highlighted, click on Replace to replace one occurrence of the word. To replace all occurrences of the word, click on Replace All, so it is changed wherever it appears in the text.

Note: Clicking Find Next twice in succession allows you to skip an occurrence of the word without replacing it.

3. INSERT TAB

Tables Section
Setting up Tables

Click on the Table section under the INSERT tab.

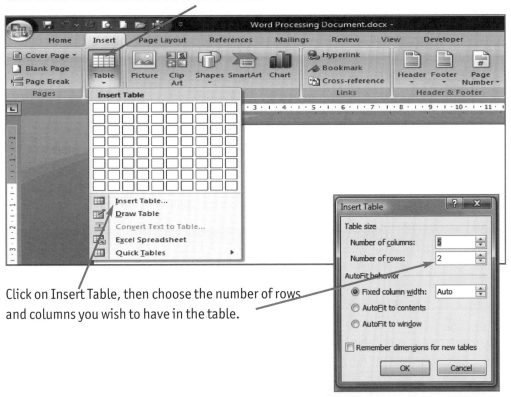

Click on Insert Table, then choose the number of rows
and columns you wish to have in the table.

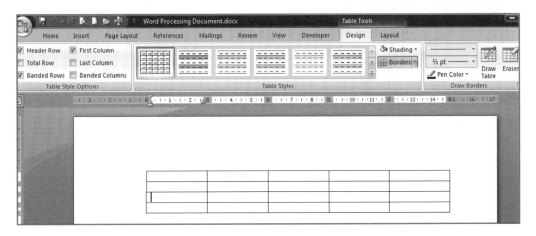

Changing Column Width in a Table

Rest the mouse I-beam on the column divider. The I-beam changes to a left/right arrow shape. Then click and hold this shape.

Drag the left/right arrow to the left to reduce the column width and to the right to widen the column width.

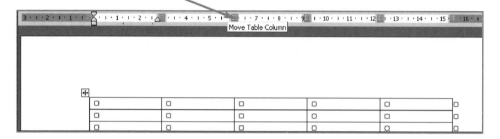

Inserting Rows in a Table

When you insert a table, the TABLE TOOLS tabs appear on your Menu bar. One tab relates to the **design** of your table and the other relates to the **layout** of your table.

To insert rows in your table, position the cursor in the row where you want to add a new row. Select the LAYOUT tab.

Then select Insert Above in the Rows & Columns section to place a row above the row you are currently in, or select Insert Below to place a row below the row you are currently in.

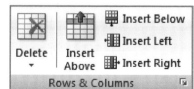

THE BASIC GUIDE TO WORD PROCESSING

OR

Position the cursor in the correct place for inserting rows above or rows below the cursor. Right click on the mouse and select Insert. Then select either Insert Rows Above or Rows Below.

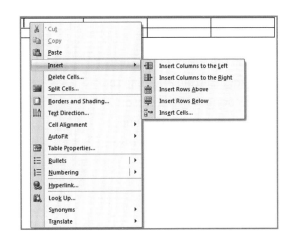

Inserting Columns in a Table

When you insert a table, TABLE TOOLS tabs appear on your Menu bar. One tab relates to the **design** of your table and the other relates to the **layout** of your table.

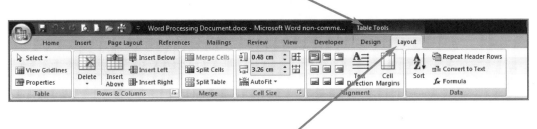

To insert a column in your table select the LAYOUT tab.

Position the cursor in the correct place for inserting columns to the left or right of the cursor.

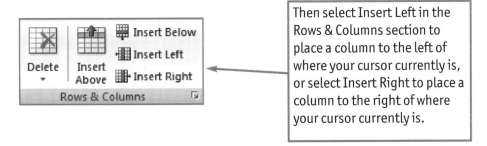

Then select Insert Left in the Rows & Columns section to place a column to the left of where your cursor currently is, or select Insert Right to place a column to the right of where your cursor currently is.

OR

Position the cursor in the correct place for inserting a column to the left or right of the cursor. Right click on the mouse and select Insert. Then select Insert Column to the Left or Insert Column to the Right.

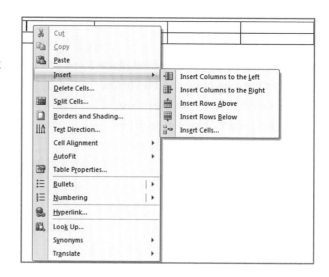

Deleting Rows or Columns in Tables

Highlight the rows (or columns) that you want to delete in the table. Select Delete in the Rows & Columns section (in the TABLE TOOLS Layout tab).

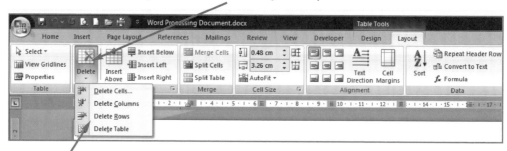

Select Delete Rows (or Delete Columns).

Changing Border Thickness in Tables

When you insert a table, the TABLE TOOLS tabs appear on your Menu bar. One tab relates to the **design** of your table and the other relates to the **layout** of your table.

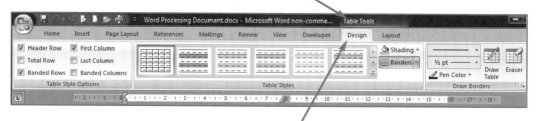

To change border thickness in tables, select the DESIGN tab.

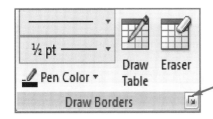

Select the cells you want to change the border thickness on. Click the arrow at the bottom corner of the Draw Borders section.

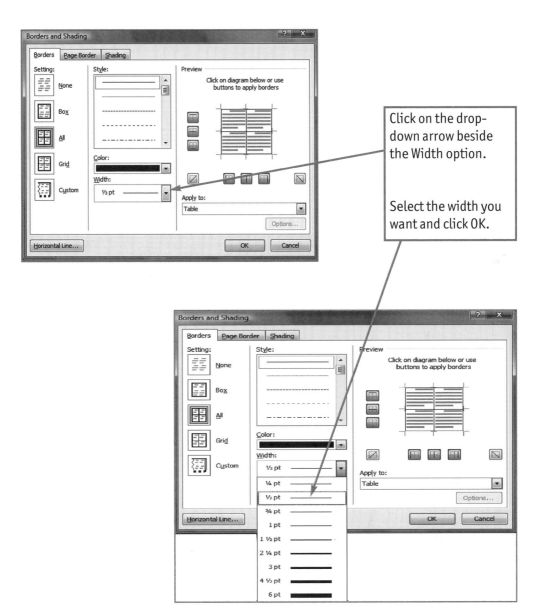

Click on the drop-down arrow beside the Width option.

Select the width you want and click OK.

Making Data Bold and Alignment in Tables

Highlight the text you want to edit and select the bold icon/alignment icons.

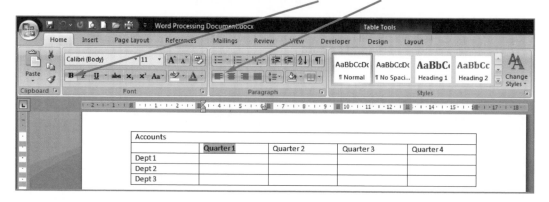

Shading in Column Headings

Highlight the cells you want to shade. In the Table Styles section of the TABLE TOOLS Design tab, select the drop-down arrow beside Shading.

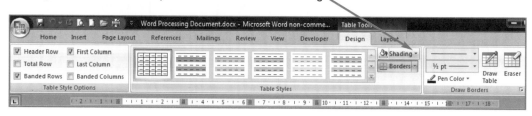

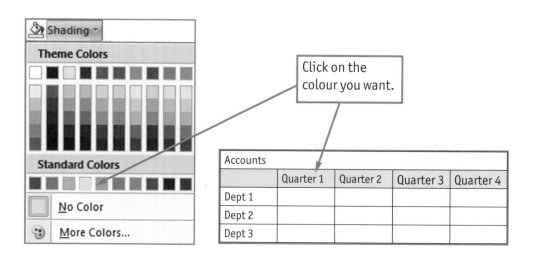

Click on the colour you want.

Merging Cells in a Table

Highlight the cells you want to merge. In the Merge Section of the TABLE TOOLS Layout tab, select Merge Cells.

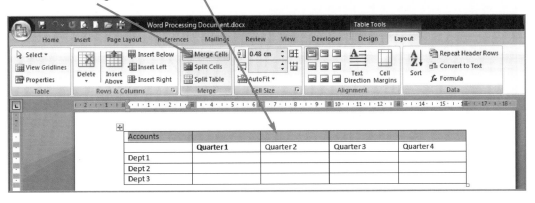

Merged cells

Accounts				
	Quarter 1	Quarter 2	Quarter 3	Quarter 4
Dept 1				
Dept 2				
Dept 3				

Sorting Data in a Table

Highlight the cells that you need to sort. Select Sort in the Data section of the TABLE TOOLS Layout tab.

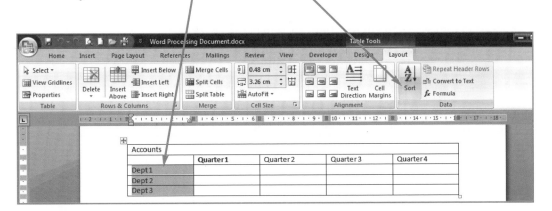

The following options menu will appear. Select the Column you want to sort by, then the Type and whether you want it in Ascending or Descending order. Then click OK.

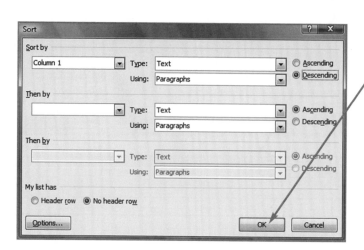

Your table will now be sorted.

Accounts				
	Quarter 1	Quarter 2	Quarter 3	Quarter 4
Dept 3				
Dept 2				
Dept 1				

Illustrations Section

Graphics

To insert graphics, use the Illustrations section of the INSERT tab.

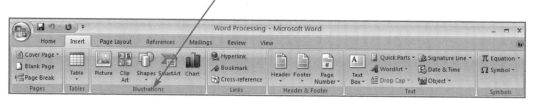

To insert a picture, select Picture and the Insert Picture screen will open.

Select the picture you wish to use and click on Insert.

To insert a clip art image, select  and the clip art panel will open on the right-hand side of your screen.

In the Search for box, type in what kind of clip art picture you want to find and click Go.

To insert a Shape, select 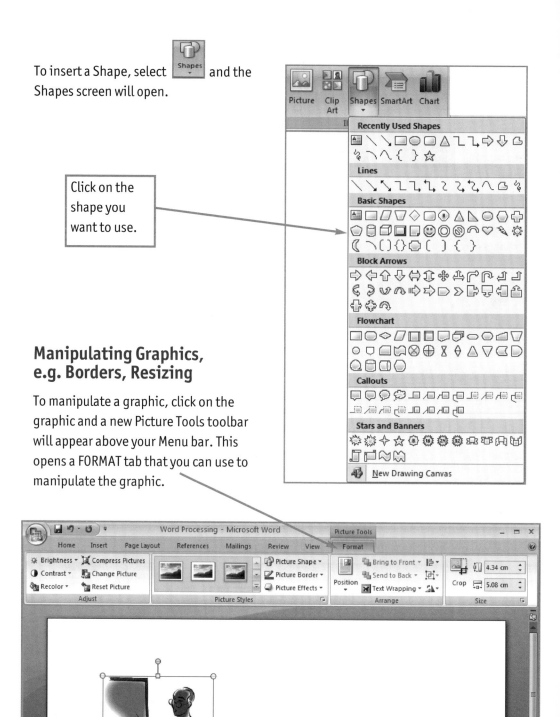 and the Shapes screen will open.

Click on the shape you want to use.

Manipulating Graphics, e.g. Borders, Resizing

To manipulate a graphic, click on the graphic and a new Picture Tools toolbar will appear above your Menu bar. This opens a FORMAT tab that you can use to manipulate the graphic.

The FORMAT tab allows you to manipulate the graphic in a number of ways.

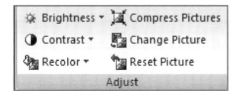 Adjust

 Picture Styles (including Borders)

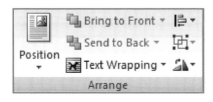 Arrange (including Text Wrapping)

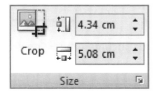 Size

Header and Footer Section

Headers and Footers

Header

In this toolbar you will find all the tools available for use in your headers and footers.
Click on the INSERT tab at the top of the Menu bar.

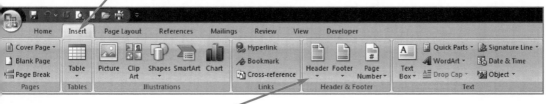

To insert a header, click on Header on the Header & Footer section.

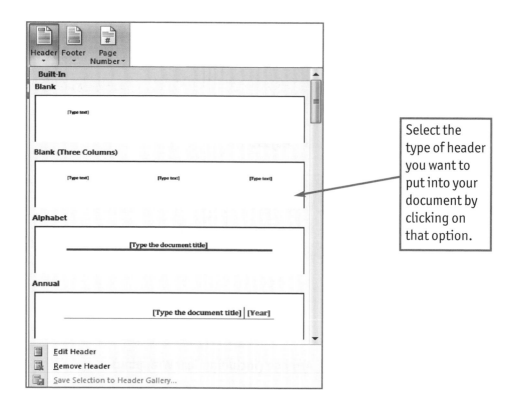

Select the type of header you want to put into your document by clicking on that option.

Once you select the type of header you want, it is inserted into your document and a new toolbar opens.

In this toolbar you will find all the tools available for use in your headers and footers.

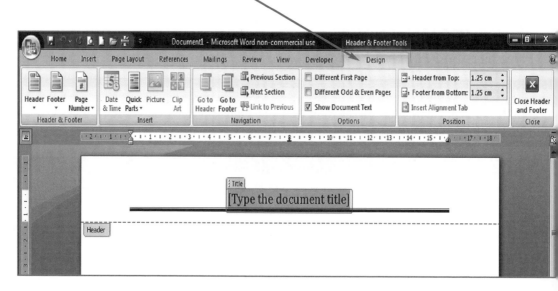

Footer

Click on the INSERT tab at the top of the Menu bar.

To insert a footer, click on Footer on the Header & Footer section.

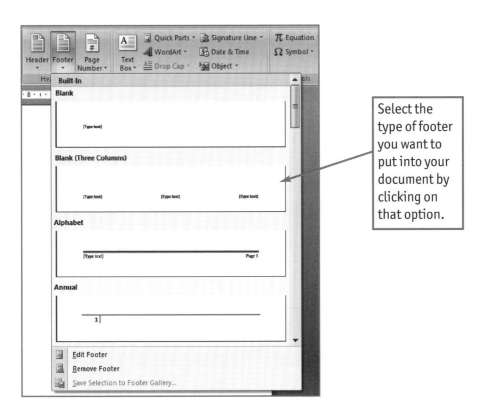

Select the type of footer you want to put into your document by clicking on that option.

Once you select the type of footer you want it is inserted into your document and a new toolbar opens.

In this toolbar you will find all the tools available for use in your header and footers.

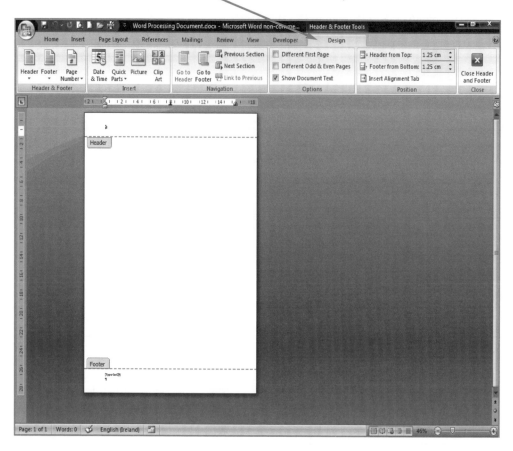

Page Numbering

Click on the INSERT tab at the top of the Menu bar.

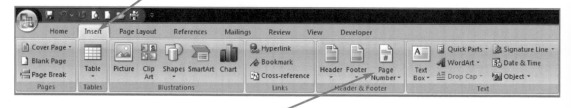

To insert page numbers, click on Page Number on the Header & Footer section.
A drop-down menu of options will appear.

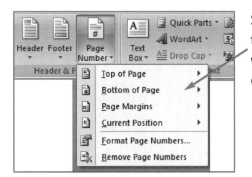

Select where you want the page numbers (i.e. top of page, bottom of page etc) and how you want to position them (i.e. left, centre, right etc).

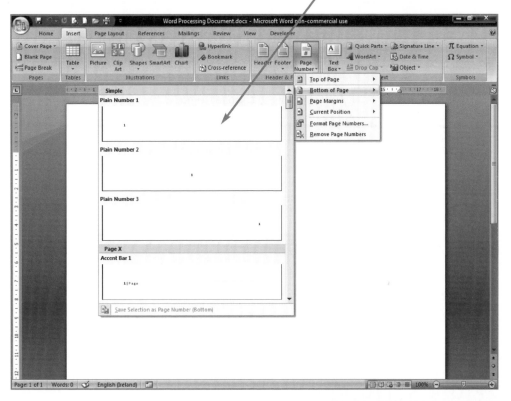

Note: You can also change the format of the page numbers by selecting Page Number Format on the drop-down menu.

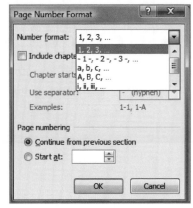

Symbols Section
International and Special Characters

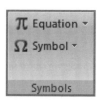

In the Symbols section under the INSERT tab click on Symbol.

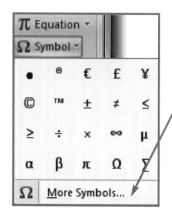

If the symbol or special character you need is not in the commonly used symbols which appear, click on More Symbols. This will give an extensive collection of symbols to choose from.

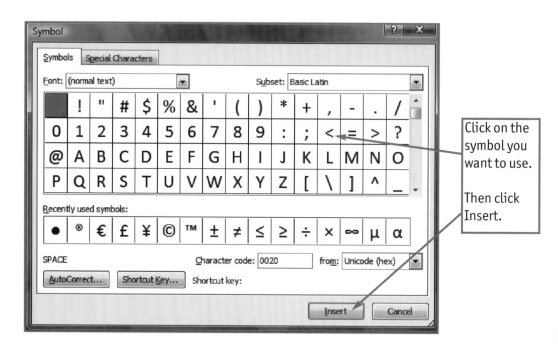

Click on the symbol you want to use.

Then click Insert.

4. PAGE LAYOUT

Page Setup Section

Indentation

1. To indent a whole block of selected text, e.g. by 2 cm.
2. Select the text you want to indent.
3. In the Paragraph section of the PAGE LAYOUT tab change the Indent setting using the arrow keys beside Left Indent.

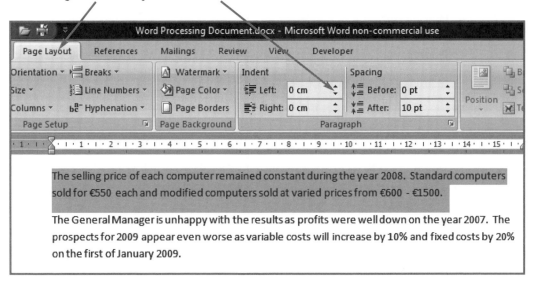

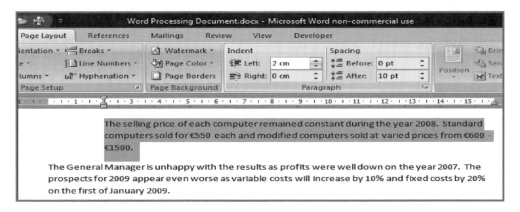

The selected text now starts 2 cm from the left-hand margin. (To indent from the right as well, increase the setting to 2 cm, using the arrow keys of the Right Indent.)

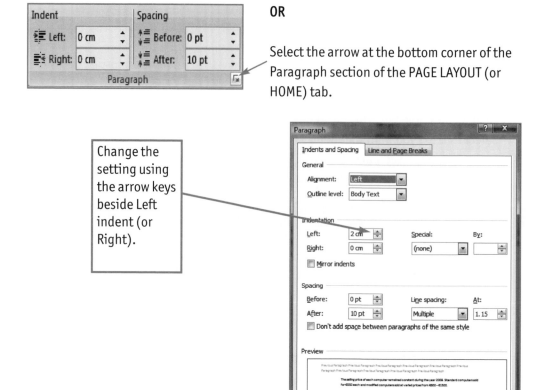

OR

Select the arrow at the bottom corner of the Paragraph section of the PAGE LAYOUT (or HOME) tab.

Change the setting using the arrow keys beside Left indent (or Right).

Page, Section and Column Breaks

Inserting Page, Column and Section Breaks

In the Page setup section under the PAGE LAYOUT tab, click on Breaks.

A drop-down list of Break options will appear. Click on the type of break you want to use in your document.

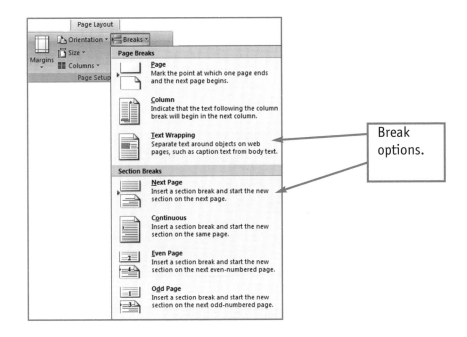

Break options.

Columns

Producing Text in Multiple Columns

In the Page setup section under the PAGE LAYOUT tab click on Columns.

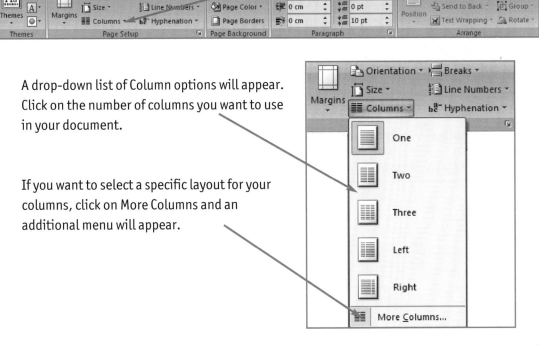

A drop-down list of Column options will appear. Click on the number of columns you want to use in your document.

If you want to select a specific layout for your columns, click on More Columns and an additional menu will appear.

5. MAILING

Start Mail Merge Section

Mail Merge and Labels

In the MAILING tab select Start Mail Merge in the Start Mail Merge section.

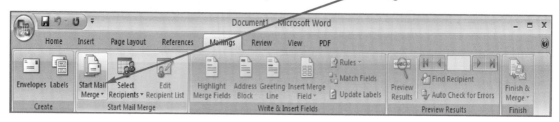

In the drop-down menu select Step by Step Mail Merge Wizard.

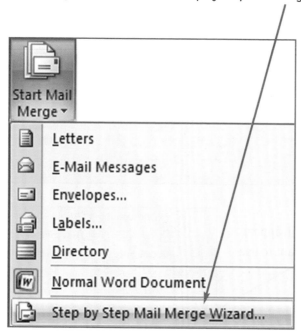

THE BASIC GUIDE TO WORD PROCESSING

A Mail Merge Wizard will open on the right of your screen.

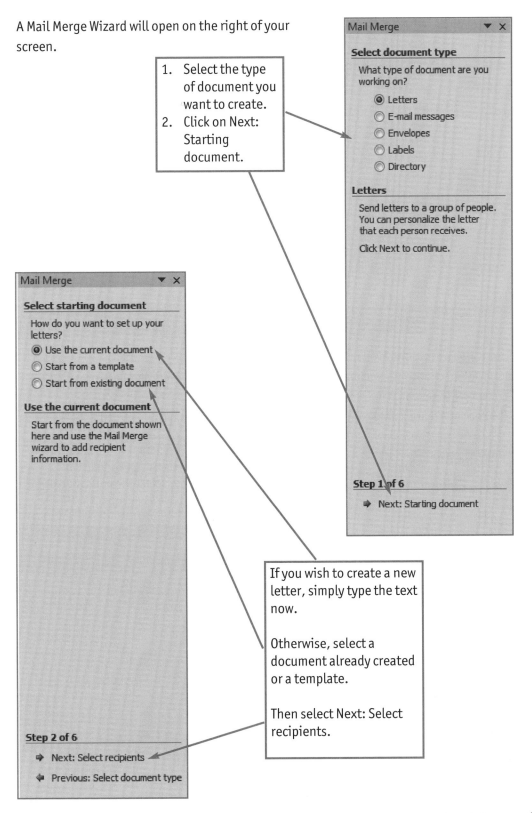

1. Select the type of document you want to create.
2. Click on Next: Starting document.

Mail Merge ▼ ✕

Select document type

What type of document are you working on?

⊙ Letters
○ E-mail messages
○ Envelopes
○ Labels
○ Directory

Letters

Send letters to a group of people. You can personalize the letter that each person receives.

Click Next to continue.

Step 1 of 6

➡ Next: Starting document

Mail Merge ▼ ✕

Select starting document

How do you want to set up your letters?

⊙ Use the current document
○ Start from a template
○ Start from existing document

Use the current document

Start from the document shown here and use the Mail Merge wizard to add recipient information.

Step 2 of 6

➡ Next: Select recipients
⬅ Previous: Select document type

If you wish to create a new letter, simply type the text now.

Otherwise, select a document already created or a template.

Then select Next: Select recipients.

Example

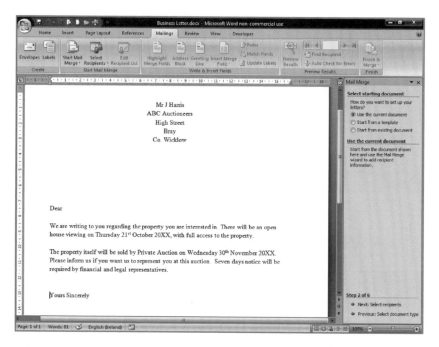

There are two options available to you:

1. You can choose the recipients of the mail merge letter from a database or spreadsheet you have already created.
2. You can create a data source of recipients if you do not have one already.

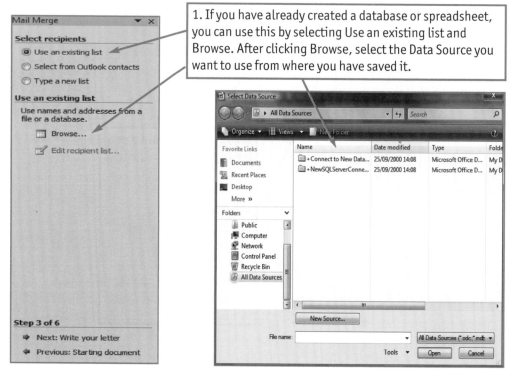

1. If you have already created a database or spreadsheet, you can use this by selecting Use an existing list and Browse. After clicking Browse, select the Data Source you want to use from where you have saved it.

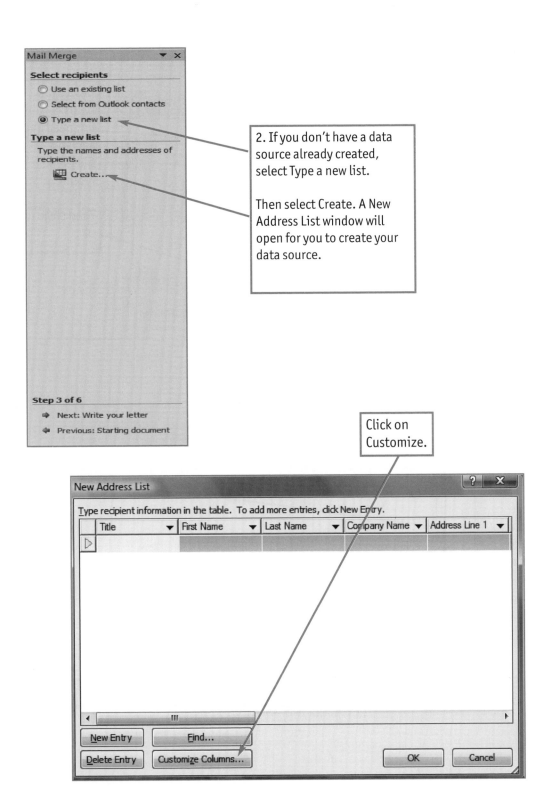

Mail Merge ▾ ✕

Select recipients

◯ Use an existing list
◯ Select from Outlook contacts
◉ Type a new list

Type a new list

Type the names and addresses of recipients.

🖳 Create...

2. If you don't have a data source already created, select Type a new list.

Then select Create. A New Address List window will open for you to create your data source.

Step 3 of 6

➥ Next: Write your letter
⬱ Previous: Starting document

Click on Customize.

New Address List ? ✕

Type recipient information in the table. To add more entries, click New Entry.

	Title ▾	First Name ▾	Last Name ▾	Company Name ▾	Address Line 1 ▾
▷					

New Entry Find...

Delete Entry Customize Columns...   OK   Cancel

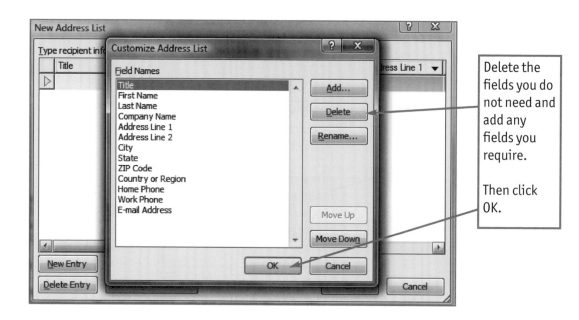

Delete the fields you do not need and add any fields you require.

Then click OK.

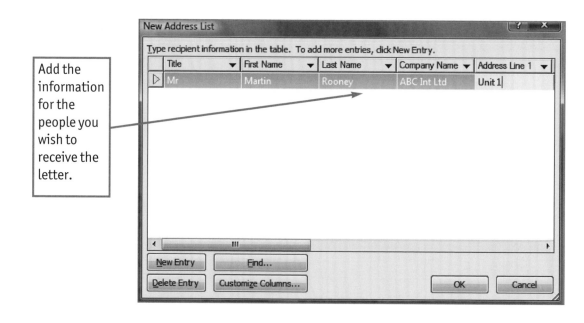

Add the information for the people you wish to receive the letter.

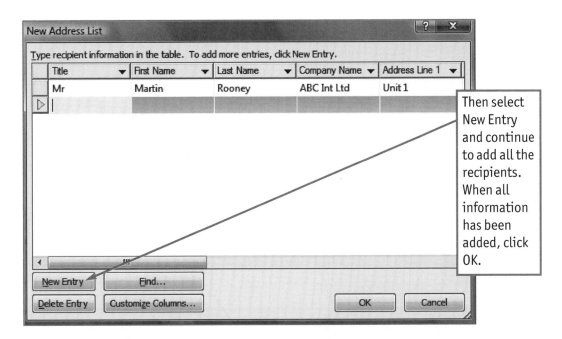

Then select New Entry and continue to add all the recipients. When all information has been added, click OK.

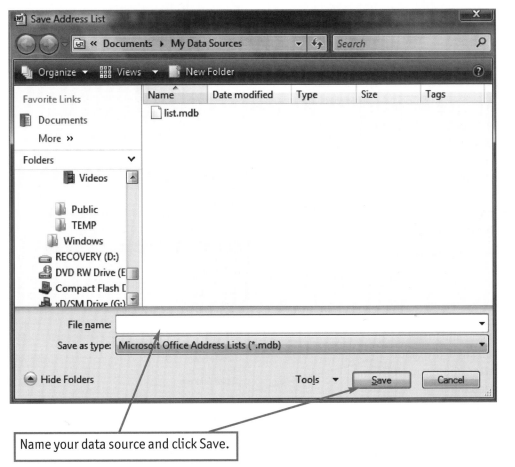

Name your data source and click Save.

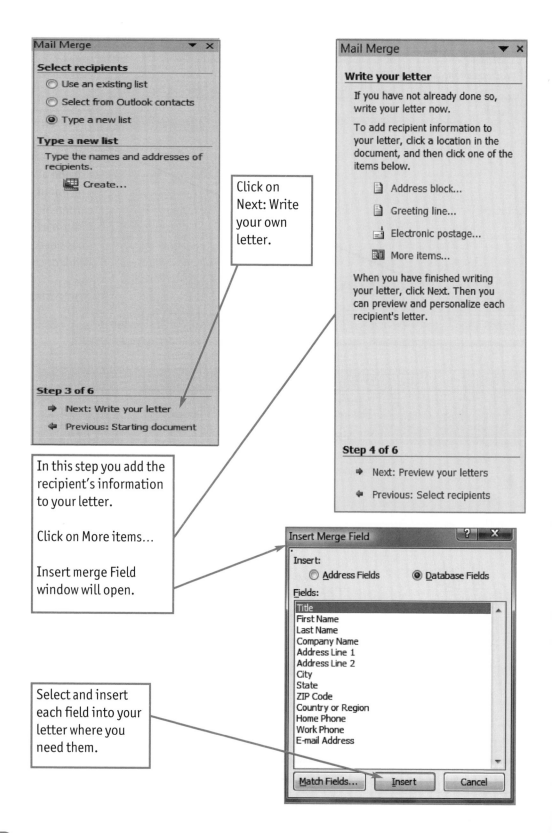

Mail Merge ▼ ✕

Select recipients

○ Use an existing list

○ Select from Outlook contacts

◉ Type a new list

Type a new list

Type the names and addresses of recipients.

▦ Create...

Click on Next: Write your own letter.

Step 3 of 6

➡ Next: Write your letter

⬅ Previous: Starting document

Mail Merge ▼ ✕

Write your letter

If you have not already done so, write your letter now.

To add recipient information to your letter, click a location in the document, and then click one of the items below.

▤ Address block...

▤ Greeting line...

▣ Electronic postage...

▦ More items...

When you have finished writing your letter, click Next. Then you can preview and personalize each recipient's letter.

Step 4 of 6

➡ Next: Preview your letters

⬅ Previous: Select recipients

In this step you add the recipient's information to your letter.

Click on More items...

Insert merge Field window will open.

Insert Merge Field ? ✕

Insert:

○ Address Fields   ◉ Database Fields

Fields:

    Title
    First Name
    Last Name
    Company Name
    Address Line 1
    Address Line 2
    City
    State
    ZIP Code
    Country or Region
    Home Phone
    Work Phone
    E-mail Address

Select and insert each field into your letter where you need them.

Match Fields...   Insert   Cancel

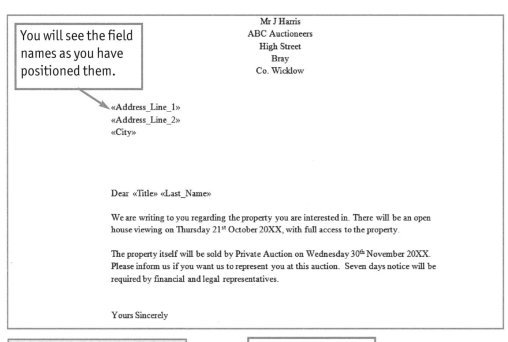

You will see the field names as you have positioned them.

Mr J Harris
ABC Auctioneers
High Street
Bray
Co. Wicklow

«Address_Line_1»
«Address_Line_2»
«City»

Dear «Title» «Last_Name»

We are writing to you regarding the property you are interested in. There will be an open house viewing on Thursday 21st October 20XX, with full access to the property.

The property itself will be sold by Private Auction on Wednesday 30th November 20XX. Please inform us if you want us to represent you at this auction. Seven days notice will be required by financial and legal representatives.

Yours Sincerely

Step 4 of 6

➡ Next: Preview your letters

⬅ Previous: Select recipients

Then click on Preview to preview your letters.

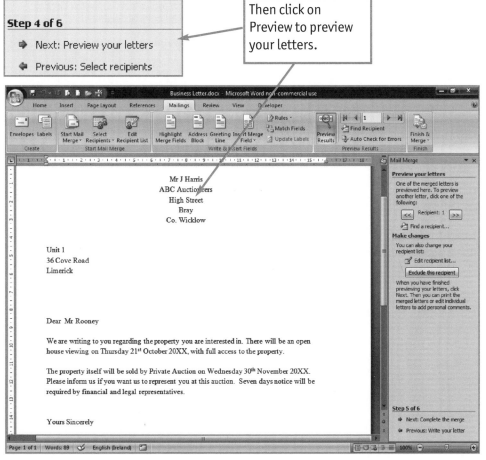

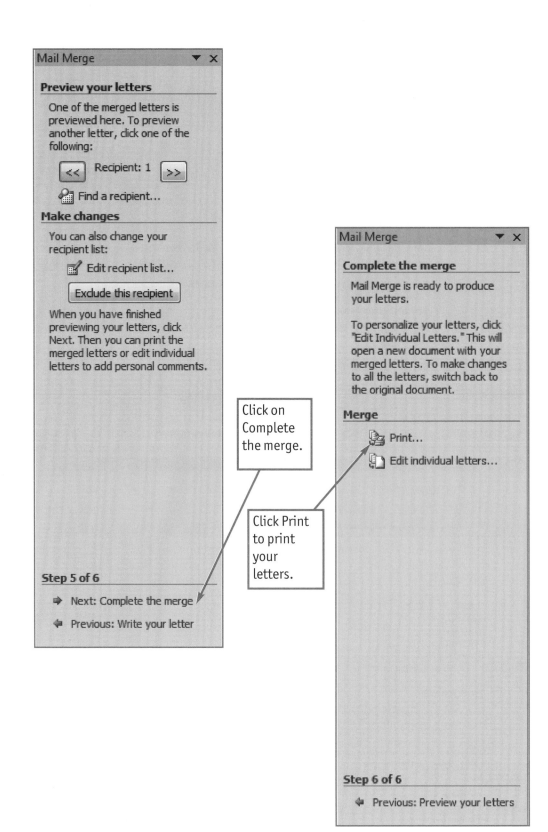

Mail Merge ▼ ×

Preview your letters

One of the merged letters is previewed here. To preview another letter, click one of the following:

<< Recipient: 1 >>

Find a recipient...

Make changes

You can also change your recipient list:

Edit recipient list...

Exclude this recipient

When you have finished previewing your letters, click Next. Then you can print the merged letters or edit individual letters to add personal comments.

Step 5 of 6

➡ Next: Complete the merge

⬅ Previous: Write your letter

Click on Complete the merge.

Click Print to print your letters.

Mail Merge ▼ ×

Complete the merge

Mail Merge is ready to produce your letters.

To personalize your letters, click "Edit Individual Letters." This will open a new document with your merged letters. To make changes to all the letters, switch back to the original document.

Merge

Print...

Edit individual letters...

Step 6 of 6

⬅ Previous: Preview your letters

6. REVIEW

Proofing Section
Proofing Tools

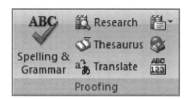

In the proofing section under the REVIEW tab there are a number of proofing tools: Spelling and Grammar, Research, Thesaurus, Translate, Translation Tip Screen, Set Language and Word Count.

 Spelling & Grammar: This allows you to check your document for spelling and grammar mistakes. Lines appear under words or sentences in your document which are spelt incorrectly or where incorrect grammar has been used. Select the Spelling & Grammar icon to go through the document and correct these mistakes.

 Research: When you select this icon, the Research pane opens on the right-hand side of your screen. It allows you to look up a variety of research and reference services such as dictionaries, encyclopedias and translation services.

 Thesaurus: Select the word you want to use in the thesaurus, then select the Thesaurus icon. The Research pane opens on the right-hand side of your screen giving a list of suggestions of other words with a similar meaning to the word you selected in your text. You can then replace your original word with one of these suggestions, if preferred.

 Translate: This allows you to translate your text into a different language.

 **Translation ScreenTip:** When you select this icon, you can turn on the ScreenTip. When you pause your cursor on a word, a text box appears over the word giving you the translation of that word in your chosen language.

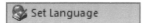 **Set Language:** Select the language you want to use to check the spelling and grammar in your document.

 **Word Count:** When you select Word Count, a text box appears on your screen telling you the number of Words, Characters, Paragraphs and Lines in your document. Word Count can also be seen on the status bar at the bottom of your page.

7. VIEW

Document Views Section
Screen Views

To change the screen view (this only changes the way the document looks on the computer screen) simply click on the screen view options in the Document View section of the VIEW tab.

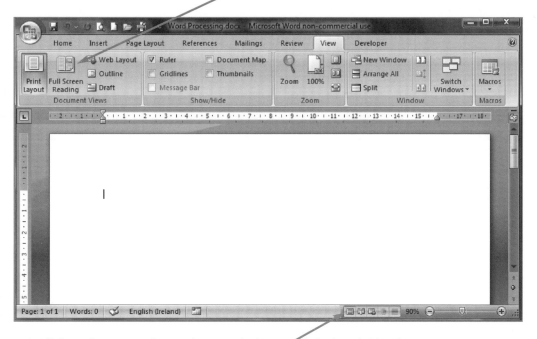

Or click on the screen view options on the bottom right-hand side of your screen. The options available are:

 Print Layout

 Full Screen Reading

 Web Layout

 Outline

 Draft

There is also the option to view the screen at different sizes by changing the zoom from 10% to 500%.

Show/Hide Section

Ruler

To show the ruler on your screen, go to the VIEW tab and tick the Ruler box in the Show/Hide section.

THE BASIC GUIDE TO WORD PROCESSING

8. FILE MANAGEMENT

Folders and Subfolders
Setting up a Folder or a Subfolder on a Drive

Make sure the USB key is in the drive.

Select the Start icon, then Computer, then USB key (removable disk).

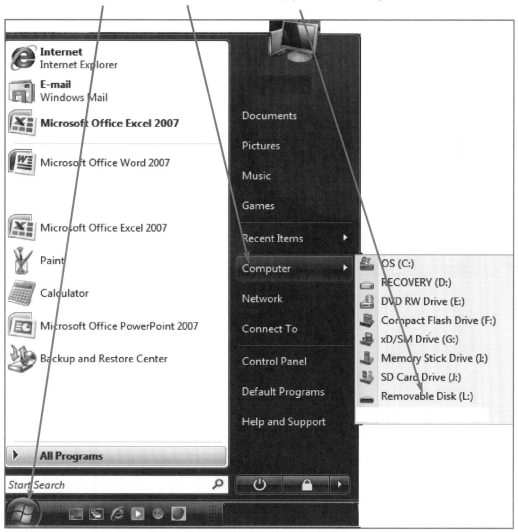

Select Organize, select New Folder (alternatively place cursor in right-hand panel and right click on the mouse to select new folder).

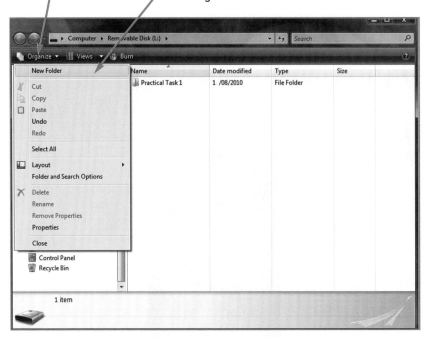

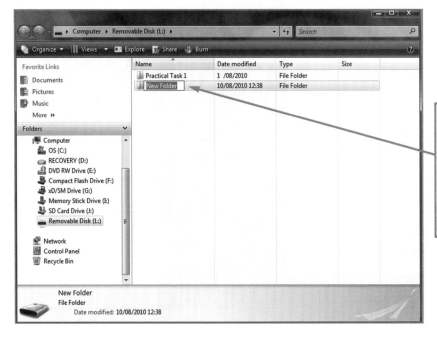

Name the New Folder by typing in the highlighted box.

To set up subfolders on a drive, click on the new folder that has been made and repeat what you have just done to create a New Folder (i.e. a folder inside another folder is known as a subfolder). Name the new subfolder.

Copying and Renaming Files and Folders

Copying a File or Folder

Select the file or folder that you want to copy and click on the Organize drop-down arrow on the toolbar and select Copy.

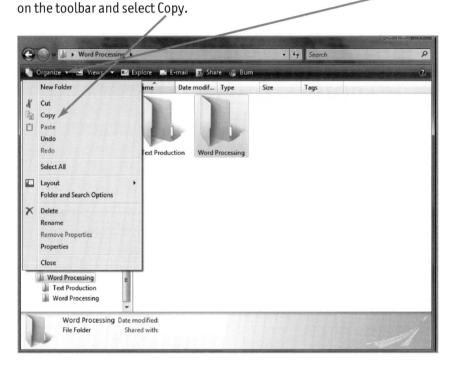

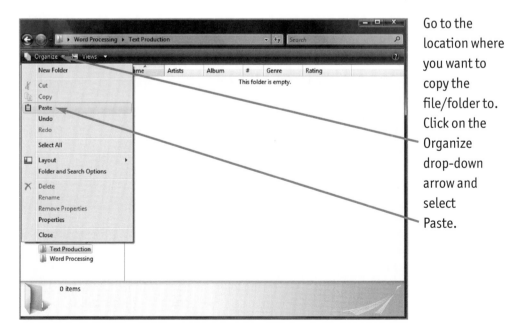

Go to the location where you want to copy the file/folder to. Click on the Organize drop-down arrow and select Paste.

Renaming Files or Folders

Right click on the folder or file you want to rename and select Rename from the drop-down menu that appears. Name the New Folder by simply typing in the highlighted box.

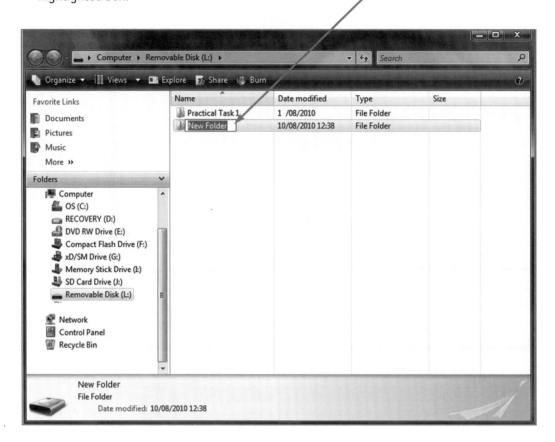

File Information

Click on the Start icon. Select Computer and select where your file is stored.

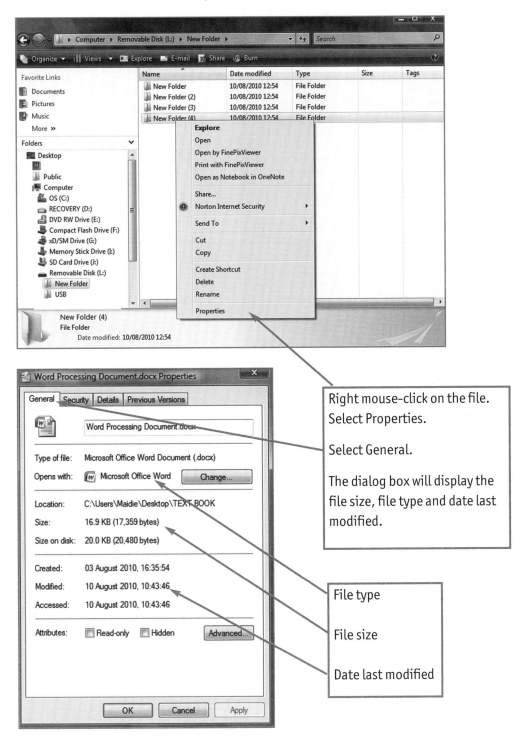

Right mouse-click on the file. Select Properties.

Select General.

The dialog box will display the file size, file type and date last modified.

File type

File size

Date last modified

Search Facility

To search, select the Start icon and type what you are searching for into the Search box.

Using the Help Facility

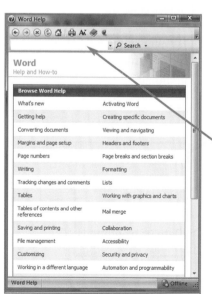

The Help Facility in MS Word 2007 is located on the top right-hand side of the screen.

Click on the blue and white question mark and the Help menu will appear.

Simply type what you want help with into the Search box and click Search.

TTTP 1	*Accepted Rules for Spacing Before and After Punctuation*

Action	Symbol	Rule
Full stop	.	No space before and one space after (traditionally two spaces after)

Example

Fiona went to a rock concert. She had a great time. Fiona met all her friends there. It was one of the best concerts this year.

Question mark	?	No space before and one space after (traditionally two spaces after)

Example

Where are you going on holidays? When are you going? Why did you choose to go there? How are you going to travel? Who are you bringing on holidays with you? What sites have you planned to visit on holidays?

Exclamation mark	!	No space before and one space after (traditionally two spaces after)

Example

This is just the beginning! Wow, that is a beautiful dress! Help! Help! Ouch! Watch out! Stop! Don't take for ever!

Comma	,	No space before and one space after

Example

We watched the aeroplane in the sky, until we could see it no longer. Jane had pizza, chips and a cola for lunch. Yesterday evening after college, Áine, Katie and Eleanor went to the cinema. Ciara Dolan lives on Dock Road, Co. Cork. When the postman arrived, Sally had already left for work.

Semicolon	;	No space before and one space after

Example		
Her house is located by the sea, though; Guiding you through the history of the Burren; with videos, catalogues, booklets and photos.		

Colon	:	No space before and one space after

Example		
Admission: Adults: €20, Children: €10. Sports activities include: tennis, squash, badminton, basketball and volleyball. Apartment layout as follows: entrance hallway, living room, kitchen, utility, 2 bedrooms and bathroom. Seasons: spring, summer, autumn and winter.		

Hyphenated word	-	No space before and no space after

Example		
Re-examined the paper. Ground-floor apartment. Deep-sea experience. Part-time job. Sea-World characters. Telephone number: 086-573553. A photo-journalist's career depends on getting the best possible photographs. Brother-in-law. E-mail address.		

Dash	—	One space before and one space after

Example		
July – September. Sunday: 2 pm – 5 pm. It requires a group of qualified people to put a newspaper together – editor, journalists, correspondents and graphic designers.		

Oblique or Solidus	/	No space before and no space after

Example		
Photos/illustrations/video displays. And/Or. On/Off. Saturday/Sunday/Monday.		

Open and closed brackets (Parentheses)	( )	One space before and no space after an open bracket and no space before and one space after a closed bracket

Example		
(1), (2), (3), (4) (a), (b), (c), (d)		

Open and closed quotation marks (inverted commas)	" "	One space before and no space after open quotation mark and no space before and one space after a closed quotation mark

Example		
"What do you want for your birthday?" asked Sean. "I want an iPod" said Aidan. "Where should we go tonight?" asked Laura. "We should go to the movies," replied John. "Great!" shouted Laura.		
Apostrophe	'	**No space before and no space after an apostrophe in the middle of a word**
Example		
The boy's trousers are too small for him. Who's taking you to the cinema? What's the matter with you? Her husband's jacket was stolen at the football match.		
Percentage	**%**	**No space between number and sign**
Example		
There will be an increase in salary for 20% of staff. Shauna achieved 95% in her Grade 6 Piano examination.		
Underline Rule	**Never underline punctuation marks unless it is in the middle of a sentence where the whole sentence is being underlined.**	
Example		
TV and Film Production. Washing Instructions: Wash similar colours together. Do not soak or bleach. Dry Flat. Cool iron on reverse.		

Correct Abbreviations and Punctuation for Measurement, Weight, Money and Time Measurement

Measurement

Abbreviation used only with figures	Meaning	Punctuation Rule – no punctuation used in metric abbreviations	Example
mm m km	Millimetre(s) Metre(s) Kilometre(s)	No punctuation, leave one space between numbers and related units of measurement	8 mm x 12 mm 3 m x 60 m 23 km x 55 km
in ft	Inch(es) Foot (feet)	No punctuation, leave one space between numbers and related units of measurement	3 in x 2 in 5 ft x 6 ft

Weight

Abbreviation used only with figures	Meaning	Punctuation Rule – no punctuation used in metric abbreviations	Example
g kg	Gramme(s) Kilogramme(s)	No punctuation, leave one space between numbers and related units of measurement	1,000 g 6 kg
oz lbs	Ounce(s) Pound(s)	No punctuation, leave one space between numbers and related units of measurement	3 oz 2 lbs

Money

Abbreviation used only with figures	Meaning	Punctuation Rule	Example
€	Euro currency	No space between sign and number	€12, €150, €280 €5.20, €60.40, €95.50 €1,000, €1,200, €5,600
£	Pounds sterling	No space between sign and number	£12, £150, £280 £5.20, £60.40, £95.50 £1,000, £1,200, £5,600
$	Dollars	No space between sign and number	$12, $150, $280 $5.20, $60.40, $95.50 $1,000, $1,200, $5,600

Time

Abbreviation	Meaning	Punctuation Rule	Example
am or a.m.	Before noon (*ante meridiem*)	Lower case, used only with figures, one space after number, with or without punctuation and no space between "am" or "a.m."	6 am or 6 a.m. 11 am or 11 a.m.
pm or p.m.	After noon (*post meridiem*)	Lower case, used only with figures, one space after number, with or without punctuation and no space between "pm" or "p.m."	9 pm or 9 p.m. 4 pm or 4 p.m.
24 hours	24-hour clock	No punctuation	1540 hours 2230 hours 0930 hours
12 hours	12-hour clock	Insert full punctuation	11.30 am or 11.30 a.m. 2.40 pm or 2.40 p.m. 12.00 pm or 12.00 p.m.

NOTE:

Lower case "x" is often used to indicate "by" or "multiplied by". One space should be left before and after the "x"; for example, 5 metres by 3 metres may be keyed in as 5 x 2 metres or 5 m x 3 m.

The following abbreviations do not require the addition of "s" in the plural: m, mm, cm, kg, in, oz.

NOTE:

Aligning figures: As a general rule, figures should align to the left. Units must come under units, e.g. tens under tens, hundreds under hundreds. This alignment in tabular work and tables is done through the use of decimal tabs.

Formulae in tables: Basic calculations can be performed in Word by placing the cursor in the cell where the calculation is required and clicking the layout tab and the formula button. In the formula dialog box enter the appropriate formula.

TTTP
3

Abbreviation Rules

Note: Acceptable Abbreviations

Abbreviation	Explanation	Example
NB	*Nota bene* – note well	NB: Keep away from fire
e.g.	*Exempli gratia* – for example	Computer technology, e.g. laptop
i.e.	*Id est* – that is	Lower case, i.e. small letter
viz. or viz	*Videlicet* – namely	The currency used, viz euros
etc.	*Et cetera* – and others	Oranges, apples, pears, etc.
Ms	Title substituted for Mrs or Miss	Dear Ms Molloy
Mr	Mister	Dear Mr Molloy
Mrs	Title for a married woman	Dear Mrs Molloy
Messrs	*Messieurs* – gentlemen	Messrs
Esq.	Esquire	Thomas Smith, Esq.
ad lib	*Ad libitum* – at pleasure	Ann made up jokes *ad lib*
no. or nos	Number(s)	No. 22 College Road, Galway
%	Per cent	Last year 20% of the workforce were made redundant

Note: Text that is abbreviated in certain cases only

General	Meaning	Abbreviation Rule	Example
&	Ampersand And	The names of firms and numbers	Clarke & Sons
Bros	Brothers	The names of organisations	O'Donnell & Bros Solicitors
c/o	Care of	Addresses	c/o Kelly Office Supplies, Bridge Road, Sligo
Co.	Company	The names of companies	Blake and Co.
COD	Cash on delivery	Invoices	COD
Ltd	Limited	The names of private limited companies	Remington Fox Ltd
PLC or plc	Public limited company	The names of such companies	Walsh & Sons plc
PS	Postscript	Letters and memos	PS Return by the end of week
Ref.	Reference	Letters and memos	Ref. 1256E

Note: Abbreviations that may be retained

Retained Abbreviations	Example
Names of countries	USA, UK
Names of organisations	ESB, IDA, INTO, ASTI, TUI
Acronyms	VAT, PAYE, PRSI

 Number Rules

Note: Words should be used in the following cases

Words Used	Example
For the numbers one to ten inclusive	Eleanor bought four bars of chocolate.
At the start of a sentence	Twenty students failed their music examination.
For single fractions in a sentence	More than half the class obtained a place in college.
For time, when followed by o'clock	The tennis meeting started at nine o'clock.

Note: Figures should be used in the following cases

Figures Used	Example
For the numbers 11 and above	There were 15 players on the soccer squad.
For dates	Date of Birth: 22.08.99
For time, except when followed by the word o'clock	Make sure you arrive at 8 p.m. sharp.
For property numbers	Walsh Solicitors, 33 Sea Road, Mayo
For measurements	The dimensions of the room are 8 m x 10 m.

Apply Block, Indented and Hanging Paragraphs

Block Paragraphs

This is the most common type of paragraphing used in text. All text begins at the left margin.

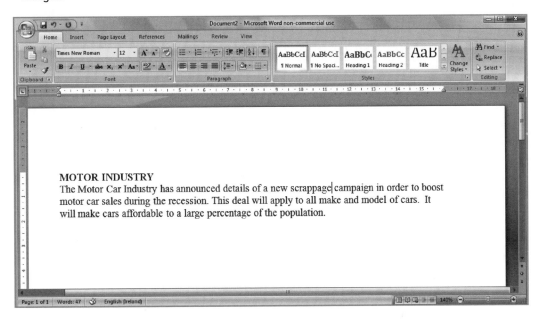

Sample of block paragraph

MOTOR INDUSTRY

The motor car industry has announced details of a new scrappage campaign in order to boost motor car sales during the recession. This deal will apply to all makes and models of cars. It will make cars affordable to a large percentage of the population.

Indented Paragraphs

The start of the paragraph is indented by approximately 1.27 cm in the first line of the text.

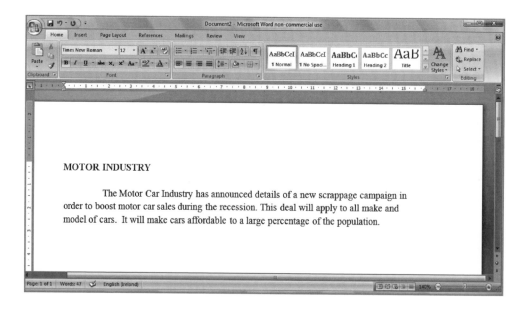

Sample of indented paragraph

MOTOR INDUSTRY

The motor car industry has announced details of a new scrappage campaign in order to boost motor car sales during the recession. This deal will apply to all makes and models of cars. It will make cars affordable to a large percentage of the population.

Hanging Paragraphs

The start of the paragraph is approximately 0.5 cm away from the rest of the text in the first line of text.

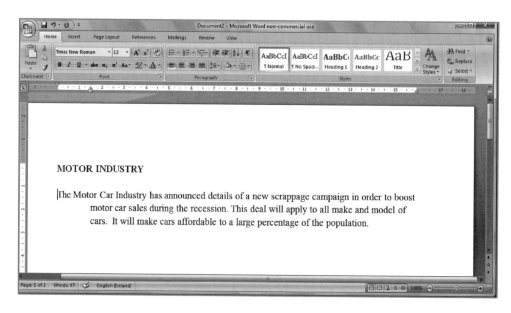

Sample of hanging paragraph

MOTOR INDUSTRY

The motor car industry has announced details of a new scrappage campaign in order to
    boost motor car sales during the recession. This deal will apply to all makes and
    models of cars. It will make cars affordable to a large percentage of the
    population.

*Use Main Headings, Subheadings, Side, Shoulder
and Paragraph Headings*

Main Headings

This appears at the top of the text and specifies the content of the text passage.

Sample styles

BLOCK CAPITALS (Bold & Centre)

> **INTERIOR DESIGN**

S P A C E D   C A P I T A L S (Bold & Centre)

> **I N T E R I O R   D E S I G N**

Subheadings

This appears within the text passage and is used to divide up the content of the text.

Sample styles

BLOCK CAPITALS

> COLOUR SCHEME

Initial Capitals and <u>underline</u>

> <u>Colour Scheme</u>

Side Headings

These are inserted at the side of the main part of the text.

Style of text
Side Headings in BLOCK CAPITALS style

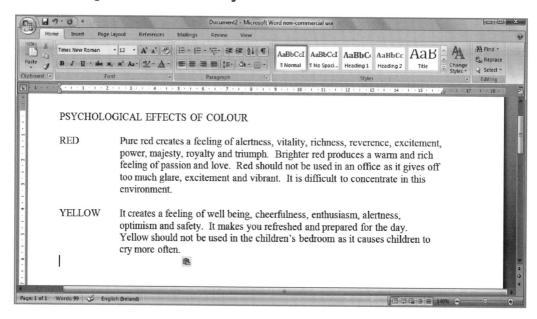

Sample of side headings in block capitals

PSYCHOLOGICAL EFFECTS OF COLOUR

RED   Pure red creates a feeling of alertness, vitality, richness, reverence, excitement, power, majesty, royalty and triumph. Brighter red produces a warm and rich feeling of passion and love. Red should not be used in an office as it gives off too much glare, excitement and vibrancy. It is difficult to concentrate in this environment.

YELLOW   It creates a feeling of well-being, cheerfulness, enthusiasm, alertness, optimism and safety. It makes you refreshed and prepared for the day. Yellow should not be used in children's bedrooms as it causes children to cry more often.

Side Headings in Initial Capitals and <u>Underlined</u> Style

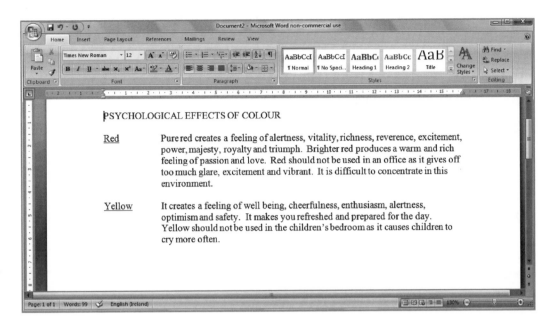

Sample of side headings in initial capitals and underlined

PSYCHOLOGICAL EFFECTS OF COLOUR

<u>Red</u>   Pure red creates a feeling of alertness, vitality, richness, reverence, excitement, power, majesty, royalty and triumph. Brighter red produces a warm and rich feeling of passion and love. Red should not be used in an office as it gives off too much glare, excitement and vibrancy. It is difficult to concentrate in this environment.

<u>Yellow</u>   It creates a feeling of well-being, cheerfulness, enthusiasm, alertness, optimism and safety. It makes you refreshed and prepared for the day. Yellow should not be used in children's bedrooms as it causes children to cry more often.

Shoulder Headings

These are inserted over passages of text where you want to divide up the content into different categories.

Style of text
Initial Capitals and <u>underline</u>.

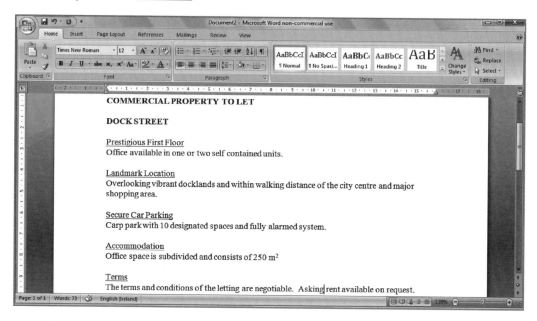

Sample of shoulder heading with initial caps and underline

COMMERCIAL PROPERTY TO LET

DOCK STREET

<u>Prestigious First Floor Office</u>
Available in one or two self-contained units.

<u>Landmark Location</u>
Overlooking vibrant docklands and within walking distance of the city centre and major shopping area.

<u>Secure Car Parking</u>
Car park with 10 designated spaces and fully alarmed system.

Accommodation
Office space is subdivided and consists of 250 m^2.

Terms
The terms and conditions of the letting are negotiable. Asking rent available on request.

Paragraph Headings

These headings are incorporated into the paragraph.

Style of text
Initial Capitals and <u>underline</u>

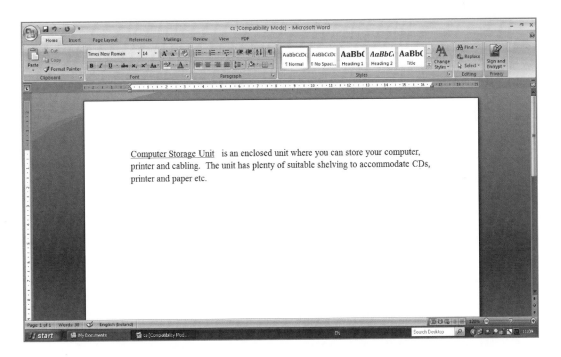

Sample of paragraph heading with initial capitals and underline

<u>Computer Storage Unit</u> is an enclosed unit where you can store your computer, printer and cabling. The unit has plenty of suitable shelving to accommodate CDs, printer and paper, etc.

A gap of approximately 0.5 cm is left between the heading and associated text.

The paragraph heading is part of the text and the heading is underlined or capitalized, with one character space left after the heading.

Sample of paragraph heading with initial capitals and underline
with one character space left after the heading

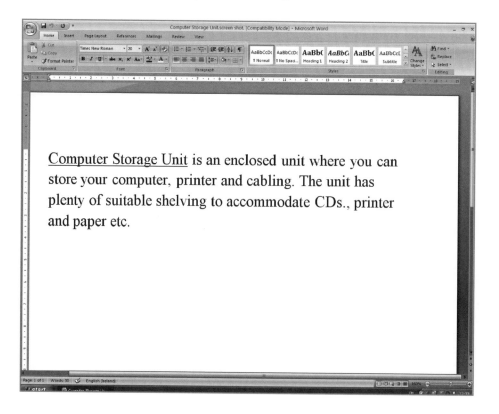

<u>Computer Storage Unit</u> is an enclosed unit where you can store your computer, printer and cabling. The unit has plenty of suitable shelving to accommodate CDs, printer and paper etc.

Standard Correction Signs for Amending Text

Symbol	Meaning	Example
♪ or ♂ or ⁊	delete	take it out
◡	close up	print as o ne word
♪	delete and close up	close up
∧ or ＞ or ∧	caret	insert here ⎯⎯ (something
#	insert a space	put one here
eg#	space evenly	space evenly ∧ where indicated
stet	let stand	let marked text stand as set
tr	transpose	change order the
/	used to separate two or more marks and often as a concluding stroke at the end of an insertion	
[	set farther to the right	too far to the right
]	set farther to the left	too far to the left
⌒	set as ligature (such as æ)	encyclopaedia
=	align horizontally	alignment
‖	align vertically	‖ align with surrounding text
x	broken character	imperfect
□	indent or insert em quad space	
¶	begin a new paragraph	
ⓈⓅ	spell out	set 5 lbs. as five pounds
cap	set in CAPITALS	set nato as NATO
sm cap or s.c.	set in SMALL CAPITALS	set signal as SIGNAL

Symbol	Meaning	Example
lc	set in lowercase	set *S*outh as south
ital	set in *italic*	set oeuvre as *oeuvre*
rom	set in roman	set *mensch* as mensch
bf	set in **bold**	set important as **important**
= or -/ or ≎ or /ᴴ/	hyphen	multi-agency approach
⫲N or *en* or /N/	en dash	1965–72
⫲M or *em* or /M/	em (or long) dash	Now—at last!—we know.
⌄	superscript or superior	⌄ as in πr^2
⌃	subscript or inferior	⌃ as in H_2O
⌄⌃ or ⌄⌃	centred	⌄⌃ for a centered dot in $p \cdot q$
⸜	comma	
⸝	apostrophe	
⊙	period	
; or ;/	semicolon	
: or ⊙	colon	
⸌⸍ or ⸜⸝	quotation marks	
(/)	parentheses	
[/]	brackets	
OK/?	Query to author: has this been set as intended?	
⊥ or ⊥ [1]	push down a work-up	an unintended ▮ mark
⤸ [1]	turn over an inverted letter	inve*r*ted
wf [1]	wrong font	wrong si*z*e or styl*e*

AGENDA 1   TEXT PROCESSING

Instructions:

1   Create the agenda.
2   Centre the company name and make it bold.
3   Insert the registered ® symbol from special characters after the company name.
4   Insert numeric bullets for each of the points on the agenda and set it up in double line spacing.
5   Save as Agenda1.
6   Print Agenda1.

Comptech® Ltd

Monthly Meeting scheduled for Wednesday, December 07, 20XX at 10.00 am in the Conference Room

Agenda

Apologies for absence
Minutes of previous meeting
Matters arising from the minutes
Correspondence
Financial Reports from Department Managers
HR: Absenteeism Report, Holiday Allowances, HR Initiatives
Organisational Structure: responsibilities, impact on projects, communications
Any other business
Date of next meeting

Instructions:

1   Create the agenda.
2   Centre the company name, make it bold and in font size 14.
3   Insert numeric bullets for each of the points on the agenda and set it up in double line spacing.
4   Type in two additional points as follows:
     11. Any other business
     12. Date of next meeting.
5   Save as Agenda2.
6   Print Agenda2.

Techno Lap Ltd

Management Meeting scheduled for Monday, November 28, 20XX at 9.00 am in the Daylight Lodge, Kilkenny

Agenda

Management Issues
Company meeting – content, delivery by who and when?
Press releases – when can they be sent to all staff?
Demand/Supply organisation chart and reporting structure
Product Portfolio approval
Bill of Materials
Demand/Supply directory and communication links
Business Plan
Sales/revenue update – existing business and new business
Overview on progress with Partnership alliances

Instructions:

1 Create the agenda.
2 Centre the company name, make it bold and in font size 16.
3 Using font effects, change the company name to small caps.
4 Insert square bullets from the bullets library for each of the points to be discussed under point 1 & 2 and set it up in double line spacing.
5 Save as Agenda3.
6 Print Agenda3.

Digicom Ltd

Management Meeting
Friday December 2, 20XX at 9.30 am in the Conference Room

Agenda

1 Human Resources

   ATRs
   Intranet
   E-Commerce presentation
   Training update
   Leavers' files
   Job descriptions
   Bonus/Incentives for employees

2 IT

   System admin issues
   PC's for employees

3 Quality update
4 Development projects review

Instructions:

1. Create the agenda.
2. Centre the company name, make it bold and in font size 18.
3. Set up the points in double line spacing.
4. Using cut and paste, switch the order of points as follows: point 3 switched with point 5 and point 2 moved below point 7.
5. Type in two additional points as follows: point 8 AOB and point 9 Date for next meeting.
6. Save as Agenda4.
7. Print Agenda4.

REAL LIFE INSURANCE COMPANY

Senior Management Meeting scheduled for Monday, January 9, 20XX at 11.00 am in Real Life Insurance Head Quarters Dublin.

Agenda

1.   Goals/objectives for company
2.   Communication in-house across depts. (distribution list for each project-documents/emails)
3.   ISO
4.   Planning
5.   Training
6.   Presentation to all on customer support
7.   Company presentation – into the future

Instructions:

1. Type the main heading in block capitals and bold.
2. Left align the first paragraph.
3. Centre the second paragraph.
4. Right align the third paragraph.
5. Justify the fourth paragraph.
6. Save as Alignment1.
7. Print Alignment1.

Ceramic Tiling

Ceramic wall and floor tiles are made from certain compounded or natural clays. They come in a wide variety, ranging from bright glazes to matt finishes. There is a wide variety of colour ranges to choose from and the glazes can be textured, mottled, stippled or rippled. The patterns are standard patterns but with ceramic tiles you can choose to be very adventurous in your choice of designing unique patterns.

Ceramic tiles are one of the most practical building materials ever made. They have proven their durability and flexibility over thousands of years.

Ceramic tiles in the bathroom are a very practical choice and will add to the capital value of your home. Tiling is a long-term investment. Caution must be taken to ensure that the tiles you have selected are suitable for the area. Check the wear rating. Check that your tiles are suitable for a wet area, if some resistance to slip is necessary.

When a ceramic tiled floor gets wet, it becomes slippery so it is best to lay floor mats in this area. Tiles with a skid-resistant surface on a floor can reduce this tendency, but the advantages are offset by a rough surface being more difficult to clean. Ceramic tiling is cleaned with bathroom detergents and a damp cloth.

1   *Type the following:*

MONDAY
TUESDAY
WEDNESDAY
THURSDAY
FRIDAY
SATURDAY
SUNDAY

2   *Make the following bold:*

MONDAY
WEDNESDAY
FRIDAY
SUNDAY

3   *Underline the following:*

TUESDAY
THURSDAY
SATURDAY

4   *Centre the following:*

MONDAY
WEDNESDAY
FRIDAY

5   *Make the following italic:*

TUESDAY
SATURDAY
SUNDAY

6   *Right align the following:*

TUESDAY
THURSDAY
SUNDAY

7   *Save as Basic Formatting1.*

8   *Print Basic Formatting1.*

1   Type the following:

January

February

March

April

May

June

July

August

September

October

November

December

2   Put all months in double line spacing.

3   Change the following to Arial and font size 16:

January

March

June

September

November

4   Centre the following:

February

May

September

December

5   Right align the following:

April

July

November

6 *Make the following bold:*
January
March

7 *Underline the following:*
September
October
December

8 *Save as Basic Formatting2.*
9 *Print Basic Formatting2.*

Instructions:

1. Use bold, italics, font size 14 and Arial style for the heading.
2. Change the numeric style bullets to alphabetic style bullets.
3. Highlight the following words in the task: timber flooring, long-lasting and wear and tear.
4. Use spell check.
5. Save as Bullets1.
6. Print Bullets1.

Suitable floor finishes for the main hall floor is heavy-duty timber for the following reasons:

1. Timber flooring is a very practical choice for a heavy-usage public area.
2. Warm, comfortable and has a welcoming look and feel.
3. It is durable and long-lasting.
4. Requires very little maintenance and is capable of taking wear and tear.
5. Extremely safe for large traffic.
6. Wide selection of timbering available.
7. Great return on investment as it lasts for years.

Instructions:

1   Use bold, italics, block capitals, font size 16 and Cooper black style for the main heading.
2   Use bold, italics, underline, font size 14 and Cooper black style for the subheadings.
3   Change the numeric style bullets to alphabetic style bullets.
4   Put the following words in the task in italics:
     clean, image, variety, low, hygienic, safety, coloured and classy.
5   Use spell check.
6   Save as Bullets2.
7   Print Bullets2.

Kitchen and Toilet Walls and Floors

Ceramic wall tiles – Kitchen and Toilets

1   Easy to clean.

2   Looks great and gives an expensive image to the place.

3   Great variety of tiles available.

4   Very low maintenance.

5   Hygienic.

Ceramic floor tiles – Kitchen and Toilet

1   Durable, suitable for heavy duty usage.

2   Very low maintenance.

3   Easy to clean, by wiping with a damp cloth.

4   Hygienic.

5   Non-slip safety tiling suited to public areas.

6   Wide range of tiling available in patterned, plain, coloured or textured.

7   Classy and expensive look and feel.

Instructions:

1 *Use bold, italics, block capitals, font size 16 and Arial black style for the heading.*
2 *Use alphabetic bullet style.*
3 *Put the following words in the task in italic:*
   boiler, stove and storage.
4 *Using cut and paste, switch point (c) with point (a).*
5 *Use spell check.*
6 *Save as Bullets 3.*
7 *Print Bullets 3.*

Forms of heating as follows:

a) Solid fuel heating: stove, open fire and boiler heated system.

b) Oil heating: radiator, stove and boiler.

c) Gas heating: radiators, fires, storage heaters and boilers.

Instructions:

1   *Use bold, italics, block capitals, font size 16 and Arial black style for the heading.*
2   *Use alphabetic bullet style.*
3   *Put the following words in the task in italic:*
     boiler, shed and building.
4   *Using cut and paste, switch point (c) with point (a).*
5   *Use spell check.*
6   *Save as Bullets4.*
7   *Print Bullets4.*

Description of Oil Heating

This is a system where the water is heated by oil fuel. The oil is contained in a tank approximately 1,000 litres, outside the building. The motor boiler, enclosed as a shed, is operated by electricity.

The motor is switched on and the water in the radiators is heated by the oil fuel. The temperature in the radiators is controlled by the thermostat. It can be regulated to a range whatever temperature levels required.

The best means of heating is to have all radiators on in each room of the building at a low level. This is also the most economical.

The internal hot water cylinder in the building is automatically also heated, which provides a constant flow of hot water for the taps.

Instructions:

1. *Type the main heading in block capitals, make it bold and centre it.*
2. *Type the subheading in block capitals and left align.*
3. *Use shoulder headings style.*
4. *Run spell check.*
5. *Click the show and hide icon to check returns and spaces.*
6. *Put a page break before "Colour Harmony".*
7. *Save as Heading1.*
8. *Print Heading1.*

PSYCHOLOGICAL EFFECTS OF DIFFERENT COLOURS

PURE PURPLE

- Royalty, richness, religious significance, instability and uneasiness.

PASTEL TINT

- Restful, soothing, soft, sedative and romantic.

SUGGESTION

Try pastel tint purple in a teenager's bedroom; the pastel tint purple with a flat finish on large expanses (walls) and a dark colour for accents of deep purple on the covers, seat etc. and light wood floors. This produces an environment of restfulness, for lazing about listening to music. It's warm, comforting, soothing and suitable for a teenage hang out.

Purple should not be used in a kitchen, as it produces a relaxing atmosphere and not a workable environment.

C O L O U R   H A R M O N Y

Colour harmony is what is achieved when the use of colour is pleasing to the eye. Visual balancing of colours provides an effect of pleasantness and a sense of well-being. It is a combination of colour and balancing the use of the colour, for example, the value and charm of colours, if used in equal steps in a colour scheme, will be harmony.

Different Types of Harmony

Analogous Harmony — Colours adjacent to each other on the colour wheel. Selection of one of the colours as a dominant theme and accent with the other analogous hues. Example, the oranges and reds of autumn leaves.

Instructions:

1   *Type the main heading in block spaced capitals, make it bold and centre it.*
2   *Type the subheading in block capitals and left align.*
3   *Use side heading style.*
4   *Run spell check.*
5   *Click the show and hide icon to check returns and spaces.*
6   *Save as Heading2.*
7   *Print Heading2.*

COLOUR HARMONY

Colour harmony is what is achieved when the use of colour is pleasing to the eye. Visual balancing of colours provides an effect of pleasantness and a sense of well-being. It is a combination of colour and balancing the use of the colour, for example, the value and charm of colours, if used in equal steps in a colour scheme, will be harmony.

Different Types of Harmony

Analogous Harmony   Colours adjacent to each other on the colour wheel. Selection of one of the colours as a dominant theme and accent with the other analogous hues. Example, the oranges and reds of autumn leaves.

Instructions:

1 *Type the main heading in block capitals, make it bold and centre it.*
2 *Type the subheading in block capitals and left align.*
3 *Use shoulder headings style, type in initial capitals and underline.*
4 *Run spell check.*
5 *Click the show and hide icon to check returns and spaces.*
6 *Save as Heading3.*
7 *Print Heading3.*

COLOUR SCHEMES

Different Types of Colour Schemes

Analogous Scheme

This scheme uses two or three adjacent colours on the colour wheel.

Complementary Scheme

This scheme combines two colours with hues directly across the colour wheel from each other.

Split Complementary Scheme

This scheme uses one hue plus the two hues on either side of the first hue's complementary hue.

Triad Scheme

This scheme uses three hues which are placed equidistant around the colour wheel.

Instructions:

1 Type the main heading in block spaced capitals, make it bold and centre it.
2 Use side heading style and type in block capitals.
3 Switch the text order. Start with the "concrete" paragraph and put the "brickwork" paragraph next.
4 Run spell check.
5 Click the show and hide icon to check returns and spaces.
6 Save as Heading4.
7 Print Heading4.

BUILDING MATERIALS

BRICKWORK	Highly durable, long-lasting and maintenance free. Any rough surfaces can be smoothed out and it can be treated with a clear finish of PVA surfaces or paint to prevent shedding of dust and grit. The brickwork can be dressed up by inserting a pattern of holes, panels of glass or other materials.
CONCRETE	Not aesthetically pleasing to the eye, it is inexpensive.
PLASTER	Not aesthetically pleasing to look at, acts as an excellent insulator and it is inexpensive.
STONE	Provides aesthetic beauty. It is very attractive, durable, requires very little maintenance. Very little expansion when it gets warm but allowance must be made for this in the joints. The stone can be polished and it has a smooth surface texture.
TILES	Aesthetically pleasing to the eye. Very practical piece to incorporate into furniture due to cleanliness, smooth finish, variety of colour and patterns can be brought to the piece of furniture.
GLASS	Variety of colouring – tinted, floated, laminated and mirrors. Can be produced in a range of thickness to suit all types of requirements for strengths and durability. The glass can be cut in a variety of shapes and sizes. Holes and patterns can also be cut out of the glass. The glass can be toughened if placed in an area prone to breakage.

Instructions:

1. Make the main heading block capitals and bold and left align.
2. Make the subheadings block capitals.
3. Use side headings style for description of each type of wood by setting up a tab at 4 cm.
4. Use initial capitals and underline the side headings and use double line spacing.
5. Using cut and paste, switch the order of woods, start with "CHERRY" and end with "BEECH".
6. Save as Heading5.
7. Print Heading5.

HARDWOODS

BEECH

Colour	Light yellow
Density	Hard, bends well, not stable, qualities of strength and durability
Grain Description	Close grained and a fine texture
Suitable Application	Wood flooring, Canadian beech is largely used in chair-making

OAK

Colour	Light cream/brown
Density	Hard fairly stable, it is not easy to work with this wood
Grain Description	Open grain, large medallury rays, silver grain
Suitable Application	High class furniture, glass cabinets, dining room table and chairs

BIRCH

Colour	Soft brown
Density	Hard
Grain Description	Regular reversed grain
Suitable Application	Plywood, chairs and general woodwork

ASH

Colour	Yellowish-white
Density	Hard, tough, bends well and stable
Grain Description	Long grain and classic qualities have made it indispensable
Suitable Application	Kitchen units, ladders and tool handles

CHERRY

Colour	Reddish, straw/pink
Density	Hard, moderately stable
Grain Description	Silky, interestingly varied
Suitable Application	Television and book cabinet, coffee table, dining room table and chairs

Instructions:

1. Make the main heading block capitals and bold, and left align.
2. Use paragraph headings style as displayed in the task. Give each paragraph heading initial capitals and underline it.
3. Using the cut and paste function, switch the order as follows: "Kitchen Lighting" as the first paragraph, next "Small Hall Lighting" and the last paragraph "Main Hall Lighting".
4. Run spell check.
5. Click the show and hide icon to check returns and spaces.
6. Change the page layout so the text appears in two columns.
7. Save as Heading6.
8. Print Heading6.

SUITABLE LIGHTING REQUIREMENTS

<u>Main Hall Lighting</u>: Evenly spaced spotlights on to the stage area are necessary to provide the perfect viewing. Coloured lighting also provides the necessary variety and an uplifting feel to the stage. Fluorescent lighting is suitable for the spectator area which is required at the beginning of the show for seating, and at intervals for safety reasons. Exit lighting is also required under fire and safety regulations, highlighting the exits in case of emergency. Side wall lights, evenly spaced along both sides of the main hall, are necessary during intervals. By equipping the main hall with a mixture of soft lighting and fluorescent, bright lighting, the main hall can be used for a wide variety of events, such as musical performances, plays, shows, lectures, assembly meetings and bingo.

<u>Kitchen Lighting</u>: Fluorescent lighting is suitable for the kitchen area in order to ensure that the place is kept clean and hygienic at all times. It is essential to have this high quality full-beamed lighting where food is prepared. For safety reasons, it is also necessary where staff are using sharp utensils, cooking equipment and breakables.

<u>Small Hall Lighting</u>: Fluorescent lighting here allows this room to be used for training purposes, evening classes with small groups etc. This lighting provides the necessary ergonomics required for running courses/meetings and meets standard health and safety requirements.

Instructions:

1 Type the main heading in block capitals, make it bold and centre it.
2 Type the subheading in block capitals and left align.
3 Use shoulder headings style.
4 Run spell check.
5 Click the show and hide icon to check returns and spaces.
6 Save as Heading7.
7 Print Heading7.

PSYCHOLOGICAL EFFECTS OF DIFFERENT COLOURS

GREEN

PURE GREEN
- calmness, sedation, muted, tranquillity, friendliness and freshness

GREEN WITH HIGH YELLOW CONTENT
- biliousness

SUGGESTION

Pale green in the study. A pale green cool mid-tone and neutral on the large expanse (wall) and light wood floors, and silver accent for the work bench, drawers, lamp, bin, with white curtains and seat cover. This environment produces a cool, refreshing and calming effect and is ideal for concentration. The size of the room increases when this colour is applied to the walls, which gives a feeling of spaciousness, openness and comfort. The sunlight shining in the window of the room adds to the freshness of the atmosphere.

Dark green should not be used in a nursery. It is too cold and dreary and would have the effect of scaring the baby.

Instructions:

1 Type the main heading in block capitals, make it bold and centre it.
2 Use side heading style with initial capitals and underline.
3 Using cut and paste, switch the order. Start with the first floor side heading and end with the ground floor side heading.
4 Run spell check.
5 Click the show and hide icon to check returns and spaces.
6 Save as Heading8.
7 Print Heading8.

DESCRIPTION OF DETACHED THREE BED-ROOMED RESIDENCE

Ground Floor

Hall (18'8" x 7'2") Wooden floor. Coving. Wood panelling on walls. Guest Toilet (6'4" x 2'6") WC, wash hand basin; walnut floor.
Living Room (32'10" x 14'5") Bay window with curtains and blinds. Ornate coving. Marble gas fire place. Carpet floor. Kitchen dining room (26' 6" x 16' 0") Cream, country-style units. Granite worktop. Dining area: three Velux windows. Walnut floor. Double doors to garden.

First Floor

Master bedroom (14'9" x 15'9"). Carpet floor. Built-in wardrobes.
Window to front, with blinds and curtains. Bathroom en suite with corner bath and shower.
Bedroom 2 (18'7" x 12'0") double. Carpet floor. Built in wardrobe. Bedroom 3 (11'8" x 17'2") double. Carpet floor. Built in wardrobe. Main bathroom (4'8" x10'2") WC, wash hand basin and shower unit. Fully tiled.

Instructions:

1 Type the main heading in block capitals, make it bold.
2 Put the subheading in block capitals and left align.
3 Use shoulder heading style with initial capitals and underline.
4 Using cut and paste, switch the order. "Secure Car Parking" paragraph comes after the "Accommodation" paragraph.
5 Run spell check.
6 Click the show and hide icon to check returns and spaces.
7 Save as Heading9.
8 Print Heading9.

COMMERCIAL PROPERTY TO LET

DOCK STREET

Prestigious First Floor
Office available in one or two self-contained units.

Landmark Location
Overlooking vibrant docklands and within walking distance of the city centre and major shopping area.

Secure Car Parking
Car park with 10 designated spaces and fully alarmed system.

Accommodation
Office space is subdivided and consists of 250 m^2.

Terms
The terms and conditions of the letting are negotiable. Asking rent available on request.

Instructions:

1   Type the main heading in block capitals, make it bold and centre it.
2   Put the subheading in block capitals and left align.
3   Use side heading style with initial capitals.
4   Run spell check.
5   Click the show and hide icon to check returns and spaces.
6   Save as Heading10.
7   Print Heading10.

---

55 ROSEDALE, TEMPLE AVENUE, WICKLOW — ACCOMMODATION

GROUND FLOOR

Porch	(6′ 6″ x 4′ 8″) PVC door. Window with blinds. Wooden floor. Light piece.
Hall	(18′ 8″ x 7′ 2″) Wooden floor. Coving. Wood panelling on walls. Radiator.
Guest Toilet	(6′ 4″ x 2′ 6″) WC. Wash hand basin. Walnut floor.
Living Room	(32′ 10″ x 14′ 5″) Bay window with curtains and blinds. Ornate coving. Two radiators with covers. Marble gas fire place. Two centre pieces. Double doors to kitchen and double door to hallway. Carpet floor. Dado rail. Large window over looking rear garden.
Lounge/Family Room	(14′ 4″ x 13′ 10″) Solid fuel stove. Radiator with cover. Centre piece. Built-in units. Large window with curtains and blinds. Coving. Dado rail. Walnut floor.

Kitchen/Dining Room	(26' 6" x 16' 0") Cream, country-style units. Granite worktop. Aga range. Recess lighting. Large island with sunken sink, granite worktop, storage underneath. Granite splash back. Breakfast bar. Double doors to dining area. Dining area: Cathedral ceiling. Three Velux windows. Walnut floor. Double doors to garden.
Utility Room	(9' 0" x 5' 5") Tiled floor. Fitted units. Sink. Window and door to side.

FIRST FLOOR

Stairs & Landing	(15' 8" x 5' 7") Large window. Carpet floor. Wood panelling on walls. Two light pieces. Hot press. Stairs to 2nd floor.
Master bedroom	(14' 9" x 15' 9") Double. Radiator. Carpet floor. Built-in wardrobes. Window to front with blinds and curtains.
En-suite bathroom	(7' 6" x 8' 0") WC. Wash hand basin. Corner bath with shower. Marble-tiled walls and floor. Radiator. Large mirror with light. Recess light.
Bedroom 2	(18' 7" x 12' 0") Double. Carpet floor. Built-in wardrobes. Light piece.
En-suite bathroom	WC. Wash hand basin. Fully tiled. Shower unit.
Bedroom 3	(11' 8" x 17' 2") Double. Radiator. Carpet floor. Window with curtains and blinds. Coving. Built-in wardrobes.
En-suite bathroom	Fully tiled. Heated towel rail. WC. Wash hand basin. Window to rear. Shower unit.
Bedroom 4	(17' 5" x 12' 4") Double. Radiator. Carpet floor. Built-in wardrobes. Coving. Light piece.

En-suite bathroom	WC. Wash hand basin. Fully tiled. Shower unit. Heated towel rail. Window.
SECOND FLOOR	
Stairs & Landing	Carpet floor. Radiator with cover.
Bedroom 5	(14' 4" x 8' 10") Double. Carpet floor. Built-in wardrobes. Two Velux windows.
Main Bathroom	(4' 8" x 10' 0") WC. Wash hand basin. Fully tiled. Heated towel. Shower unit.
Office	(14' 4" x 6' 0") Carpet floor. Recess lighting. Built-in units. Velux window.

Instructions:

1   *Create the sender's letterhead and save it as a template.*
2   *Type this business letter using the standard full blocked and open punctuation layout.*
3   *Type your initials as the second part of the reference number and insert today's date.*
4   *Insert a New Paragraph after the sentence ending "...annual membership subscription".*
5   *Proof read and spell check the document.*
6   *Click the show and hide icons to check returns and spaces.*
7   *Save as Letter1.*
8   *Print Letter1.*

Sender's Letterhead

Rockville Hotel Leisure Club
Dawson Place
Dublin

Ref: *PW/your initials*

Insert today's date

Mr Joseph Fahy
College Street
Dublin

Dear Member

Re: Membership Renewal

Your membership of the Rockville Hotel Leisure Club is due for renewal on the 1st next month. Attached is the club brochure, which sets out the fees for the membership categories. There has been a modest increase in the annual membership subscription.

I would appreciate if you would complete and return your application with the appropriate fee as soon as possible. Fees may be paid by cash, cheque, credit card or standing order over six months (first payment upfront with five monthly payments thereafter). Should you wish to avail of the six-month payment scheme, please complete the standing order and return it with your first payment.

Yours sincerely

Patricia Walsh
Leisure Club Manager

Enc: Club brochure

Instructions:

1 Create the sender's letterhead and save it as a template.
2 Type this business letter using the standard full blocked and open punctuation layout.
3 Type your initials as the second part of the reference number and insert today's date.
4 Switch the order of paragraphs as follows: "We are seeking an explanation..." as second paragraph and "Enclosed please find a copy..." as third paragraph.
5 Change paragraph spacing to 6 points after the paragraph.
6 Justify the body of the letter.
7 Proof read and spell check the document.
8 Click the show and hide icons to check returns and spaces.
9 Save as Letter2.
10 Print Letter2.

Sender's Letterhead

Silver View Lawn Tennis Club
Sea Road
Sligo

Ref: TC/

Today's date

ESB
Willow Place
Cork

Dear Sir/Madam

ESB BILL QUERY

As there is an outstanding query on the excessive bill we received at the Silver View

Lawn Tennis Club for the ESB billing period dated June 19, 20XX amounting to €15,000. I am not in a position to settle this account until it is further investigated.

Enclosed please find a copy of the letter sent to Mary Burke, Team Leader, ESB, Willow Place, Cork dated August 13, and another letter dated June 29, 20XX. We have not had a reply or acknowledgement to either letter as yet.

We are seeking an explanation on how our ESB bill could have trebled during this period and have been promised a visit from someone in the ESB Office but as yet this has not happened. We urgently request attention in this matter.

I am enclosing a cheque amounting to €3,000 as part payment for the billing period 18 June to 9 August.

Yours sincerely

Thomas Crowe
Club Manager

Enc: Cheque

Instructions:

1   Use an appropriate layout for a business letter as shown in Letter task 1 and Letter task 2.
2   Type your initials as the second part of the reference number.
3   Insert a new paragraph after the sentence ending "…of an examination date".
4   Move the block capitals sentence to the start of the body of the letter.
5   Make the block capitals sentence bold and italics.
6   Find "candidate" and replace it with "student" in the body of the letter.
7   Proof read and spell check the document.
8   Click the show and hide icon to check returns and spaces.
9   Save as Letter3.
10 Print Letter3.

Sender's Letterhead

Local Centre Examinations Office
Music Academy
Willow Park
Dublin

Subject:	Violin Examination Schedule
Reference:	TC/
Date:	Insert today's date
Complimentary Close:	Yours sincerely
Inside Address:	Miss Mary Walsh
	Music Teacher
	Grange Road
	Cork
Salutation:	Dear Miss Mary Walsh

| Letter From: | Sandra Clarke |
| | Secretary |

| Enc: | Applicant List |

Text of letter:

Please find enclosed details concerning the examinations of your candidate(s). We would be grateful if you would contact this office immediately if you discover that any of the particulars pertaining to your candidate(s) are incorrect and require amendment.

To avoid delay, we would request that your student(s) attend for examination at the appointed time. Any candidate who does not attend at the stated time will be deemed to be absent. In the case of illness, a medical certificate is necessary to secure a credit to your account or the postponement of an examination date. Please ensure that candidates take only original copies of material into the examination room.

PLEASE NOTE THAT THE DATE AND TIME OF THE EXAMINATIONS CANNOT BE CHANGED UNLESS A MEDICAL CERTIFICATE IS SUPPLIED.

If you have any queries please do not hesitate to contact me.

Instructions:

1 Use an appropriate layout for a business letter as shown in Letter task 1 and Letter task 2.
2 Centre the sender's letterhead.
3 Insert a new paragraph after the sentence ending "… in June 20XX" and another new paragraph after the sentence ending "… polite and confident".
4 Proof read and spell check the document.
5 Click the show and hide icon to check returns and spaces.
6 Save as Letter4.
7 Print Letter4.

Sender's Letterhead

Briarhill College
Canal Lane
Wexford

Subject:	Reference
Reference:	JOL/Your own initials
Letter to:	Mr Tom Moran
	Information Systems Manager
	Comtech Ltd
	Lismore Industrial Estate
	Wexford
Date:	Today's Date
Closure:	Appropriate complimentary closure
Salutation:	Mr Tom Moran
Signatory's Name:	James O'Leary

Signatory's Title: Business Teacher

Letter:

Mr Sean Burke is currently attending the FETAC Business Computing and Internet Applications Course at Briar Hill College. This course started September 20XX and ends in June 20XX.

The subjects studied by Sean include the following: Customer Service, Communications, Spreadsheets, Databases, Information Systems, Web Authoring, Web Design, Word Processing, Internet, Spreadsheets and Book-keeping (both manual and computerized).

Sean should be capable of carrying out routine office duties that include word processing, database, spreadsheet and accounts. The programs that used in the college are Microsoft Office (Word, Access and Excel) as well as book-keeping.

Sean Burke's attendance and punctuality are satisfactory. Sean is very co-operative in class and completes his assignments on time. He has a very positive manner and gets on very well with his class mates. Sean is assertive, polite and confident. If you have any further queries, please do not hesitate to contact me. I wish Sean Burke every success in his future endeavours.

Instructions:

1   *Use an appropriate layout for a business letter as shown in Letter task 1 and Letter task 2.*
2   *Centre the sender's letterhead.*
3   *Insert a new paragraph after the sentence ending "…in April 20XX".*
4   *Find "experience" and replace with "placement".*
5   *Proof read and spell check the document.*
6   *Click the show and hide icon to check returns and spaces.*
7   *Save as Letter5.*
8   *Print Letter5.*

Sender's Letterhead

St John's Education Centre
Slane Street, Athenry, Galway

Date:	17 September 20XX
Subject:	WORK EXPERIENCE
Reference:	JG/Your own initials
Signatory's Name:	Joseph Gallagher
Signatory's Title:	Course Co-ordinator
Letter to:	Mr Mark Dunleavy
	Production Manager
	Power Tech Ltd
	River Dale Industrial Estate
	Athenry
	Galway
Closure:	Appropriate complimentary closure

Salutation: TO WHOM IT MAY CONCERN

Text of Letter:

We would be most grateful if you can accommodate our student for a period of work placement, working one day per week in your organisation/business from October 20XX to April 20XX. Work experience is a requirement for the FETAC Certificate in Business and Marketing Studies. As you can appreciate, it is of great benefit to the students to gain useful work experience in your business.

Some of the modules studied by the students include:

– Customer Service
– Communications
– Spreadsheets
– Databases
– Information Systems
– Marketing
– Internet
– Bookkeeping (both manual and computerised)

The college provides insurance cover for the students during the period of work experience.

At the end of the work experience I would be grateful if you could fill out the enclosed Supervisor's Report Form detailing the student's performance for the duration of the work experience.

If you need to clarify anything with me, feel free to email me at any time at joseph.gallagher@yahoo.co.uk or phone me at 085-2344245.

Instructions:

1. Create the minutes.
2. Make the company name bold.
3. Use tabs and tab leaders where appropriate.
4. Use multilevel bullets.
5. Insert date and page x of y in the footer.
6. Save as Minutes1.
7. Print Minutes1.

KEEGAN MANAGEMENT COMPANY LTD

Minutes of meeting held on Monday 17 January 20XX at 8.00 pm in the Seashore Hotel.

PRESENT	Mr John Walsh	(Chairman)
	Ms Irene Naughton	(Vice-Chairman)
	Jane O'Brien	(Secretary)
	Martin O'Connor	(Treasurer)
	Pat Hynes	(Public Relations)

In attendance   Peter Burke

(1) <u>Apologies for Absence</u>
Apologies were received from Mr Jim Hogan.

(2) <u>Minutes of last meeting</u>
The minutes of the last meeting held on 4 January were read, approved and signed by the Chairman.

(3) <u>Matters arising from the minutes</u>
There were no matters arising.

---

(4) Correspondence

    4.1   A letter was received from Mr John Brennan's solicitor regarding the insurance claim for damages to the ceiling and walls of his apartment.

    4.2   A quotation was received from O'Connells Painting Company for the internal and external painting of the apartment block and the outside railings.

    4.3   Letters were sent to all owners and residents of the apartment block informing them of the following; new intercom system installed and instructions on how to use it.

(5) Report from Accounts Department

Mr Paul Clarke, Treasurer, presented the audit reports to the management company. The income for the management company for this financial year exceeded the expenditure. There was a total of €5,000 remaining in the sinking fund. It was decided that this money could be used to replace the broken car park gates.

(6) Report on recent disturbance incidences on the property

Mr John Walsh provided a detailed report on the number of instances that have occurred in the apartment block over the last number of months such as burglaries, noise disturbances and parties etc. It was decided to identify the apartments that were responsible for the parties and write to the owners requesting that they deal with the problem. Follow-up phone calls also need to be made to owners within the next seven days.

(7) Any other business

Prior to closing the meeting, the Treasurer asked that all members take a copy of the Audit Report on the way out. There being no further business the meeting closed at 10.00 pm.

(8) Date of next meeting

The next meeting will take place on Monday, 21 February, 20XX.

Signed_____   Date _____

Instructions:

1. *Create the minutes.*
2. *Make the company name bold.*
3. *Use tabs and tab leaders where appropriate.*
4. *Use multilevel bullets.*
5. *Insert date and page x of y in the footer.*
6. *Save as Minutes2.*
7. *Print Minutes2.*

EUROTEL MAPPING COMPANY

Minutes of customer service meeting held on Monday 22 November 20XX at 10.00 am in the Conference Room.

PRESENT	Marcel Mathews	Technical Manager
	Siobhan Cunningham	Production Manager
	Ann Marie Waters	C S Manager
	Tom Murphy	HR Manager

In attendance   Peter Kelly

(1)   Apologies for Absence
Apologies were received from Ms Ann Butler.

(2)   Minutes of last meeting
The minutes of the last meeting held on 18 October were read, approved and signed by the Chairman.

(3)   Matters arising from the minutes
There were no matters arising.

(4)   Correspondence
    4.1   A letter was received from Head Office with regard to Company Sales for the month ending 20 September 20XX.

4.2   A letter was received from a satisfied customer with regard to the recent release of the product line for 20XX.

(5) New SMS Database
Michael Rickard, who is here on work experience for four weeks, is currently working on an Access database to replace the old SMS database. Ciaran spoke about this, saying that Michael may not finish this project within four weeks. If anyone would like to take a look at progress, Ciaran will put a copy of it up on the network. Michael is putting in drop-down menus. Only products that we have can be inputted into the database to prevent the possibility of orders with non-existent products. The database will contain all customer details. This will hopefully make deliveries and reports easier. It doesn't take Cash Collection into account, but it should be possible to print up a report saying who should be invoiced on a particular day or week. This is considered effective.

(6) New Product Releases are on schedule and the company will meet the deadlines.

(7) Communication between Technical Support and Fulfillment
It was agreed that this could be removed from future meetings, as everything seems to be going well.

(8) Any other business
There being no further business the meeting closed at 1.00 pm.

(9) Date of next meeting
The next meeting will take place on Friday 14 January 20XX.

Signed _____   Date _____

Instructions:

1　Type the main heading in block capitals and make it bold.
2　Use block paragraphing style for the first paragraph.
3　Use indented paragraph style for the second paragraph.
4　Use hanging paragraph style for the third paragraph.
5　Justify the fourth paragraph.
6　Insert your full name in the header.
7　Insert date and page x of y in the footer.
8　Run spell check.
9　Click the show and hide icon to check returns and spaces.
10　Save as Paragraphing1.
11　Print Paragraphing1.

Ceramic Tiling

Ceramic wall and floor tiles are made from certain compounded or natural clays. They come in a wide variety, ranging from bright glazes to matt finishes. There is a wide variety of colour ranges to choose from and the glazes can be textured, mottled, stippled or rippled. The patterns are standard patterns but with ceramic tiles you can choose to be very adventurous in your choice of designing unique patterns.

Ceramic tiles are one of the most practical building materials ever made. They have proven their durability and flexibility over thousands of years.

Ceramic tiles in the bathroom are very practical choice and will add to the capital value of your home. Tiling is a long-term investment. Caution must be taken to ensure that the tiles you have selected are suitable for the area. Check the wear rating. Check that your tiles are suitable for a wet area, if some resistance to slip is necessary.

When a ceramic tiled floor gets wet, it becomes slippery so it is best to lay floor mats in this area. Tiles with a skid-resistant surface on a floor can reduce this tendency, but the advantages are offset by a rough surface being more difficult to clean. Ceramic tiling is cleaned with bathroom detergents and a damp cloth.

Instructions:

1 Use an appropriate layout for this report.
2 Save as Report1.
3 Print Report1.

ROYAL ROCK GOLF CLUB
ACCIDENT REPORT FORM

1.   DATE & TIME OF ACCIDENT:

   _____

2.   EXACT LOCATION:

   _____

   _____

3.   NAME OF PERSON(S) AND RELATIONSHIP TO THE CLUB
   (MEMBER/VISITOR/STAFF):

   _____

4.   ACCIDENT DETAILS, INCLUDING DETAILS OF WITNESSESS, INJURIES, ETC.:

   _____

   _____

   _____

   _____

   _____

5.   CORRECTIVE ACTION TO BE TAKEN (IF APPLICABLE):

   _____

   _____

6.   NEED TO ADVISE THE FOLLOWING:
   Club Manager
   Board of Management

Signed : _____   Date:_____

Instructions:

1 Use an appropriate layout for this fire evacuation report.
2 Run spell check.
3 Click the show and hide icons to check returns and spaces.
4 Change the screen view to full screen.
5 Save as Report2.
6 Print Report2.

FIRE
EVACUATION PROCEDURES

It is the duty of all members of the Public on the premises to conduct themselves in such a way that no person on the premises is exposed to danger from fire through any act or omission of theirs.

If you discover a FIRE, report its location immediately to a member of the staff and follow instructions.

If you hear the FIRE ALARM:

1. **DO NOT Panic.**

2. **Follow the instructions of STAFF regarding evacuation.**

3. **DO NOT run. Walk quietly to the nearest exit to which you are directed.**

4. **Once outside the building, DO NOT re-enter in any circumstances.**

5. **DO NOT congregate or cause obstruction to the FIRE BRIGADE.**

FIRE

EVACUATION PROCEDURES IN THE EVENT OF FIRE TO BE OBSERVED BY ALL MEMBERS AND STAFF

1. Should you discover a FIRE or one is reported to you, IMMEDIATELY sound the ALARM and

2. Open the nearest available exit in your zone and in an authoritative voice direct the Public to the exit by calling "THIS WAY OUT PLEASE".

3. Make sure that all areas in your zone, i.e. Toilets/Rooms are searched for stragglers. If safe to do so, close all doors and windows behind you.

4. Once evacuated, no person should be allowed back into the building in any circumstances.

5. Report to the FIRE SAFETY OFFICER at the ASSEMBLY POINT and advise him/her of the situation.

FIRE ACTION

ON DISCOVERING A FIRE

1. Alert other people and staff immediately and call the Fire Brigade on 999. Advise the Manager or the most senior person available pending arrival of the Fire Brigade.
2. Attack the fire, if possible using the appliances provided but also ensuring not to take any risks.
3. Proceed to the assembly point, which is located near the entry to the car park.

KNOW:

A. Your means of escape, primary and secondary.
B. The nearest fire appliance and how it should be used.
C. The assembly point.

In the event of a Fire:

A. Maintain silence.
B. Leave the premises without stopping to collect your belongings, without rushing and without attempting to pass others.
C. Do not return to the building for any reason unless authorised to do so.

Instructions:

1   Create the following signage.
2   Select an A4 portrait page.
3   Type "DAYS HOTEL LEISURE CLUB" in font size 14, Veranda style and centre it.
4   Type "JOB VACANCY: PART-TIME GYM ATTENDANT" on the second line, in font size 14, Veranda style and centre it.
5   Type "We are currently seeking to recruit a Part-Time Gym Assistant who will be responsible for assisting the Fitness Manager in the running of the Fitness Club between 6 pm and 10 pm each evening, Thursday to Monday" on the next line as the body of the advertisement, in font size 12, Veranda style. Use justify alignment.
6   Type "The Ideal Candidate will have the following:" on the next line as a heading in font size 12, Veranda style and left align.
7   Using square bullets, type the following bullet points in font size 12, Veranda style: "previous experience in a similar role desirable" , "excellent interpersonal and communication skills", "strong people management skills", "enthusiastic and motivated individual", "ability to work on own initiative", "strong team skills".
8   Type "Please apply online with details of relevant experience", on next line in font size 12, Veranda style and left align.
9   Save as Advertisement1.
10 Print Advertisement1.

Instructions:

1   Insert your full name in the header.
2   Insert the date and page x of y in the footer.
3   Run spell check.
4   Click the show and hide icon to check returns and spaces.
5   Save as Header&Footer1.
6   Print Header&Footer1.

Ceramic Tiling

Ceramic wall and floor tiles are made from certain compounded or natural clays. They come in a wide variety, ranging from bright glazes to matt finishes. There is a wide variety of colour ranges to choose from and the glazes can be textured, mottled, stippled or rippled. The patterns are standard patterns but with ceramic tiles you can choose to be very adventurous in your choice of designing unique patterns.

Ceramic tiles are one of the most practical building materials ever made. They have proven their durability and flexibility over thousands of years.

Ceramic tiles in the bathroom are very practical choice and will add to the capital value of your home. Tiling is a long-term investment. Caution must be taken to ensure that the tiles you have selected are suitable for the area. Check the wear rating. Check that your tiles are suitable for a wet area, if some resistance to slip is necessary.

When a ceramic tiled floor gets wet, it becomes slippery so it is best to lay floor mats in this area. Tiles with a skid-resistant surface on a floor can reduce this tendency, but the advantages are offset by a rough surface being more difficult to clean. Ceramic tiling is cleaned with bathroom detergents and a damp cloth.

Instructions:

1. Use bold, block capitals, font size 16 and Arial black style for the heading.
2. Use numeric bullet style.
3. Insert an image from clip art or a picture from the internet.
4. Using cut and paste, switch point (I) with point (III).
5. Use spell check.
6. Save as Image1.
7. Print Image1.

Textures

    I. Wood
       (insert an image of wood)

    II. Carpet
       (insert an image of carpet)

    III. Brick
       (insert an image of brick)

    IV. Stone
       (insert an image of stone)

Instructions:

1   Create the following signage.
2   Select bevel from the basic shapes and enlarge it to fill an A4 landscape sheet.
3   Type "PLEASE" in font size 80, Calibri style and centre it.
4   Type "Keep Canteen" on the second line, in font size 80, Calibri style and centre it.
5   Type "Area Tidy" on the third line, in font size 80, Calibri style and centre it.
6   Select a dark green background colouring and select white for the text colouring.
7   Insert an appropriate image from clip art at the bottom of the sign.
8   Run spell check.
9   Save as Image2.
10 Print Image2.

Instructions:

1   Create the following signage.
2   Select rectangular from the basic shapes and enlarge it to fill an A4 landscape sheet.
3   Type "SPORTS DAY" in font size 60, Arial black style and centre it.
4   Type "Wednesday May 18, 20XX" on the second line, in font size 60, Arial black style and centre it.
5   Type "All are Welcome" on the third line, in font size 60, Arial black style and centre it.
6   Select a dark red background colouring and select white for the text colouring.
7   Insert an appropriate image from clip art at the bottom of the sign.
8   Run spell check.
9   Save as Image3.
10 Print Image3.

Instructions:

1 Create the following signage.
2 Select an A4 portrait page.
3 Type "SOCCER PRACTICE" in font size 72, Britannic bold style and centre it.
4 Type "Every Thursday Evening at 6.00 pm" on the second line, font size 36, Britannic bold style and centre it.
5 Type "All are Welcome" on the third line, in font size 48, Britannic bold style and centre it.
6 Select a light blue background colouring and select black for the text colouring.
7 Insert an appropriate image from clip art at the bottom of the sign.
8 Run spell check.
9 Save as Image4.
10 Print Image4.

Instructions:
1   Create the following signage.
2   Select an A4 portrait page.
3   Type "Rosemount Tennis Club Rules" on the first line, in WordArt style 11 and centre it.
4   Type "JUNIORS" on the second line, in font size 36, Arial black style and centre it.
5   Select square bullets and type all bullets in font size 14 and Arial black style and left align.
6   Run spell check
7   Save as Notice1.
8   Print Notice1.

ROSEMOUNT TENNIS CLUB RULES

JUNIORS

- **Swipe your key ring as you enter**
  (If lost, it must be replaced at a cost of €5)

- **Juniors must sign the attendance sheet and pay €1 each day**

- **No food or drink allowed in the court**

- **Proper footwear must be worn in the courts at all times**

- **All players must keep within booking times**

- **No valuables as the Club takes no responsibility for items lost or stolen**

- **Juniors to behave at all times**

- **Juniors only allowed into the Club to play racket games**

- **Juniors to be collected by 6 pm sharp**

- **Respect the property at all times**

TABLE 1   **TABS AND TABLES**

Instructions:

1   *Using tabs and tables create the following report.*
2   *Shade appropriate cells.*
3   *Save as Table1.*
4   *Print Table1.*

NAME							
ADDRESS							
CONTACT NO.							
Day/days		**Time:**	**From Date:**		**To Date:**	**No. to attend**	

NAME	
TOTAL CHARGE	
RECEIPT NO.	

Deposit of €200 (refundable if no damage caused to Club Property)	Receipt No.:		Date:	

18 yrs or under	Adults
Rules as follows:	**Rules as follows:**
<ul><li>All non-members to sign the visitors' book on entry to the Club.</li><li>Parent/Tutor supervision required.</li><li>Any damages caused to Club property to be paid to Club out of the Deposit.</li><li>Any person requested to leave the Club by Club staff must do so.</li><li>Disruptive behaviour not tolerated.</li><li>You must provide your own insurance cover while on property and submit a copy for our files.</li><li>In the event of an accident an "Accident Report" must be completed.</li><li>Respect the facilities of the Club.</li><li>Be collected from the Club after event/training.</li></ul>	<ul><li>All non-members to sign the visitors' book on entry to the Club.</li><li>Any damages caused to Club property to be paid to the Club out of the deposit.</li><li>Any person requested to leave the Club by Club staff must do so.</li><li>You must provide your own insurance cover while on property and submit a copy for our files.</li><li>In the event of an accident an "Accident Report" must be completed.</li><li>Respect the facilities of the Club.</li></ul>

I agree to adhere to the above Rules of the Club.	
Signature:	
Date:	

TABLE 2   **TABS AND TABLES**

Instructions:
1   *Create the tables below with table headings in bold .*
2   *Shade each row on the table in a different colour.*
3   *Use tabs to align the names in the "Present" section.*
4   *Insert a page number.*
5   *Save as Table2.*
6   *Print Table2.*

Minutes:	**Management Meeting**		
Date:	30 November 20XX		
Present:	David Kelly	Michael Reilly	Deirdre Burke
	Sharon Hopkins	Mary Flynn	Pat O'Toole

Action Item	Ownership	Status
Internal Reports: Monthly work schedule sheet detailing the goals and objectives of each member of the team for each month.	Each manager to provide monthly report.	Ongoing
External reports (Planning, Cost base, Quality benchmarking, Productivity/Deadlines, Customer Services)	Timeline: for discussion mid-November meeting.	
ISO	POT to provide information on ISO focus for new structure	POT to confirm meeting on 15 Nov
SMS	MF to provide update to mgt. team at next meeting	Review project plan on Intranet
Department budgets for next year	MR to provide guidelines	In process. Dec 11

TRS	MR to review in Finance/Admin	
Costing per product line/department	MR to work on this with individual managers throughout November	Ongoing
IT process improvement	SH to distribute form for IT infrastructure requirements for completion by each manager	Sent Friday 11/11/XX
Motivation	Mgt team to work on their choice of motivation initiatives for next meeting	
Christmas shutdown	Decision to be made at next meeting as to Christmas 20XX shutdown.	
Christmas vouchers	DK to research possible outlets for vouchers	
Annual leave policy	Carry over of hours to next year	Staff to be informed of remaining annual leave entitlement and encouraged to take it before year end. Carrying over of hours at each manager's discretion
H&S statement	DK to look into updating H&S statement, with H&S Officer	On hold

TABLE 3   **TABS AND TABLES**

Instructions:

1. *Use an appropriate table layout with no border.*
2. *Use a sum formula to create the total.*
3. *Centre the heading and make it bold and underline.*
4. *Make the subheadings bold and underline.*
5. *Save as Table3.*
6. *Print Table3.*

BREAKDOWN OF COSTS FOR OPEN DAY SEPTEMBER 26, 20XX	
PROMOTIONAL MATERIAL	
School drops, flyers, promotional posters	€2,000
MEDIA ADVERTISING	
Advertisements in newspaper	€350
Radio advertising on Galway Bay FM	€900
Mailing campaign (stamps, envelopes etc)	€192
Bouncing castle	€ 90
COACHING	
4 coaches	€320
Refreshments	€500
Miscellaneous prizes	€148
TOTAL	€4,500

TABLE 4   **TABS AND TABLES**

Instructions:

1   *Create the tables below with table headings in bold and shaded.*
2   *Centre the heading and make it bold and use font size 18.*
3   *Insert a page number and a date in the footer.*
4   *Save as Table4.*
5   *Print Table4.*

Communications Links – Demand/Supply

IRELAND	SUBJECT – MANAGEMENT	Salt Lake City, USA
MD Robert Bell	Planning Schedule Agreement per release Bill of Materials approval New Projects Agreement Product Portfolio Costing of Product lines Special products evaluation Problems/bottlenecks New product development Infrastructure requirements Financial concerns Company communications – Press releases, etc Link between demand and supply Sales and Marketing information provider	VP Operations – David Reilly
	REPORTS/DOCUMENTS	
Robert Bell	Planning Report– GRD and GAD per release Planning Report – Components per release Development Work Schedule Overview per month	David Reilly

IRELAND	SUBJECT – CUSTOMER SERVICES	Salt Lake City, USA
Customer Service Mgr (Fulfillment, TS, Webmaster) Tom Lawless	Project requests for Proj. Coordinator TS issues with Development TS issues with Sales Demo Requests End User titles product delivery and product issues Product release schedule Customer Orders / Delivery queries Customer queries with Sales BV Contracts cash collection Customer Care Leads Sales Back Office Support Intranet and internet requests Press Releases Contract information and status Bad Debtors Customer issues from Sales	
	REPORTS/DOCUMENTS	
Tom Lawless Monthly reports / Metrics	Monthly reports/Metrics Delivery schedules Road, Address & Webservices (fulfillment)	

IRELAND	SUBJECT – IT SYSTEMS	Salt Lake City, USA
Systems Administrator Tim Curley	Protection/security Primary/Secondary domain. IT advisory service Ongoing projects, requirements, upgrades review etc. Costing comparisons of hardware/software Spare resources between facilities – software/hardware	Martha Rowe
	REPORTS/DOCUMENTS	
Tim Curley Infrastructure requirements 20XX	Inventory logging of all hardware in use	Martha Rowe

IRELAND	SUBJECT – HUMAN RESOURCES	Salt Lake City, USA
HR Officer Sarah Madden	Job Descriptions Development employee approval for statutory leave General HR issues Development employee follow up from review feedback	David Reilly
	REPORTS/DOCUMENTS	
Sarah Madden	Absenteeism/Holidays etc., for Team Leaders Annual Performance Reviews for Development Team Organisation Chart for Development Irl. and Rotterdam Development – Changes in personnel, recruitment, training	David Reilly

IRELAND	SUBJECT – FINANCE	Salt Lake City, USA
Financial Controller Martin Griffin	Ongoing liaison on cash flow Queries on accounts	Diana Wright
	REPORTS/DOCUMENTS	
Martin Griffin	P & L and Balance Sheet Inter-company accounts reconciliation Annual Company Budget Forecast Cash flow forecast for six months Cash flow requirements on monthly basis Financial accounts year end	Diana Wright

IRELAND	SUBJECT – GEOGRAPHIC/ADDRESS ACQUISITION	Salt Lake City, USA
Production Manager Donal Quinn	GIS technical support to queries from demand	Jenny Bolton
	REPORTS/DOCUMENTS	
Donal Quinn	Release statistics Bookbuild Planning Schedule	Jenny Bolton

IRELAND	SUBJECT – QUALITY/ADDRESS	Salt Lake City, USA
Quality Manager Ann O' Leary	ISO practices & procedures (Development) Mastering of Component CDs	Jay Cotter
	REPORTS	
Ann O'Leary	ISO documentation concerning Development	Jay Cotter

TABLE 5 TABS AND TABLES

Instructions:
1. Using landscape orientation, create the tables below with table headings in bold and shaded.
2. Centre the heading and make it bold and in block capitals.
3. Use bold and block capitals for the subheadings.
4. Save as Table5.
5. Print Table5.

Planning: Demand/Supply Meeting
Management

Action Item/Topic	Description/Ownership	Timeline	Status
Business Plan	Tom currently working on the financials	2 weeks	Open
Product Portfolio	Needs to be finalised by the Board	End of month	Open
Management reporting d/s	John, Mary and Mark to create	1 month	Ongoing
Demand/Supply communication links	John, Mary and Mark to work on improvements/relationship building d/s	3 months	Ongoing
Company meetings & press releases	John, Mary and Mark to discuss	End of month	Open

Road

Action Item/Topic	Description/Ownership	Timeline	Status
Data licensing & royalty reporting for NT and TA	Jim to handover all necessary material/knowledge on data licensing & royalty reporting for NT & TA to Patrick. Do we still have a contract with TA and if so why?		Apr 22 start of handover from Fiona
New creations-Brazil and Mexico	John and Tom to review the proposals provided by Mark	End of month	Ongoing

Address

Action Item/Topic	Description/Ownership	Timeline	Status
Address Query 1.6 roll out to 2.2	Letters to be sent to the Query 1.6 clients offering them a reasonable solution	End Apr 11	Open
Address Query Sales Drive	Tom to discuss with Sales and Marketing etc.	3 weeks	Ongoing

Customer Service

Action Item/Topic	Description/Ownership	Timeline	Status
Creation of a centralised MS Access database of all clients	Ann to set up	End of month	Currently working on proposal
Customer Satisfaction	Tom to discuss with sales/mkting/product mgt a way in which customer information is fedback into a system where it can be logged, evaluated and used by operations to better satisfy the customer requirements etc. (also ISO requirement).	3 weeks	Open

Financial

Action Item/Topic	Description/Ownership	Timeline	Status
Costing per product line	John to produce costing per product line with the necessary input from Fiona and David	April/May XX	Open
Acquisition Budget 20XX	John to provide Tom with an Acquisition Budget for 20XX	19 April XX	Open
Training Budget 2XX	John provided with training budget summary for 20XX for review. It is important to note that some of this money is recoverable through a FAS grant aid (provided by the government).	End of month	Awaiting feedback

TABLE 6   **TABS AND TABLES**

Instructions:
1. *Create the table below using font size 18.*
2. *Centre the main heading, make it bold and in block capitals.*
3. *Bold, block capitals and shade the column headings.*
4. *Sort the details column in alphabetical order.*
5. *Right align Quantity, Unit Price and Total Price columns.*
6. *Insert a row at the bottom and use the sum formula to create the total price.*
7. *Run spell check.*
8. *Save as Table6.*
9. *Print Table6.*

EXAMINATION PAPERS BOOKLET PRICING LIST

QUANTITY	DETAILS	UNIT PRICE	TOTAL PRICE
5	Accounting (H) Leaving Certificate	€4.00	€20.00
8	Biology (H) Leaving Certificate	€4.00	€32.00
10	English (H) Leaving Certificate	€4.00	€40.00
3	Gaeilge (H) Including aural papers & CD Leaving Certificate	€5.00	€15.00
7	Mathematics (H) Leaving Certificate	€4.00	€28.00

TABLE 7   **TABS AND TABLES**

Instructions:

1   *Create the table below using font size 22.*
2   *Centre the main heading and make it bold and in block capitals and font size 26.*
3   *Make the column headings bold and in block capitals and shaded.*
4   *Sort the date column in alphabetical order.*
5   *Right align the amount column.*
6   *Delete the row dated "12.06.XX".*
7   *Run spell check.*
8   *Save as Table7.*
9   *Print Table7.*

Receipt for Professional Services

Date	Treatment	Amount
25.06.XX	Periodontal Treatment	€120.00
18.06.XX	Periodontal Treatment	€200.00
12.06.XX	Periodontal Consultation	€150.00
29.10.XX	Periodontal Treatment	€200.00

Received with thanks €670

Instructions:

1 Use an appropriate layout.
2 Centre the main heading and make it bold and in block caps.
3 For the column headings use initial capital, bold and shading.
4 Merge cells where necessary.
5 Right justify the times column.
6 Colour code each of the schedules in different colours.
7 Insert an additional row at the end of the "TIME" column and put in "6.00 pm 7.00 pm".
8 Save as Table8.
9 Print Table8.

Conference Room Timetable

TIME	MONDAY	TUESDAY	WEDNESDAY	THURSDAY	FRIDAY
8.00 am – 9.00 am	SALES MEETING				
9.00 am – 10.00 am		IT MEETING			HUMAN RESOURCES – INTERVIEWING SCHEDULE
10.00 am – 11.00 am					
11.00 am – 12.00 pm					
12.00 pm – 1.00 pm	CLIENT MEETING		CLIENT MEETING		
LUNCH					
2.00 pm – 3.00 pm		PRODUCTION TRAINING SESSION		INTERNATIONAL VIDEO CONFERENCING NETHERLANDS	HUMAN RESOURCES – INTERVIEWING SCHEDULE
4.00 pm – 5.00 pm	INTERNATIONAL VIDEO CONFERENCING UK				
5.00 pm – 6.00 pm					

TABLE 9　　　　　　　　　　　　　　　　　　　　　　**TABS AND TABLES**

Instructions:

1 Use an appropriate layout.
2 Centre the main heading and make it bold and underline.
3 Use bold and shading for the subheadings.
4 Sort column 1 in alphabetical order.
5 Switch column 4 "Working Qualities" with column 5 "Material Size".
6 Delete column 6 "Possible Applications".
7 Remove the gridlines of the table.
8 Save as Table9.
9 Print Table9.

METALS DESCRIPTION SUMMARY

Metals	Colour	Density	Working Qualities	Material Size	Possible Applications
Stainless Steel	Bright metal and satin.	Chromium approx. 18% and nickel approx. 8% with mild steel creates the stainless steel.	Difficult to work with, although it can be cut, bent, drilled, threaded, filed and welded. Due to the increased hardness, it requires a special process.	It is available in standard made-up tiles for surface applications.	
Aluminium	Bright metal, slate grey in colour.	Granite rock treated with caustic soda produces alumina and this is refined by electrolysis into the pure metal. It is soft and weak metal and it is low in density.	Easy to work with, as it can be welded or riveted easily. It is expensive to work on. It can be cut, riveted, bent, spun, drilled, threaded, filed, welded and cast. It is a good conductor of electricity and can be polished, acid-etched and anodised.	It can be produced in lengths of 30 metres or more.	Used for aircraft and vehicle building, also architectural glazing, windows, sliding doors, greenhouses, tubular garden furniture.
Copper	Very distinctive reddish/ brown colour.	It is low in density.	It can be polished, riveted, bent, spun, beaten, braised and soldered. Can also be used as a sheet material for surfacing or cladding.		Plumbing, efficient carrier of electricity.
Brass	Gold glow.	Surface quality of the metal is close.	It can be riveted, cast, threaded, filed and soldered.	Available in sheet form, rod, bar or angles.	Ironmongery – handles, knobs etc. Clock-making, furniture fittings and screws.

TABLE 10   **TABS AND TABLES**

Instructions:

1   Create the table below with table headings in bold.
2   Shade the top row on the table in a different colour.
3   Insert "TRANSCRIPTION EQUIPMENT" in the header.
4   Insert a page number and a date in footer.
5   Switch column "MODEL NO." with "SERIAL NO.".
6   Save as Table10.
7   Print Table10.

DICTATING/TRANSCRIBING EQUIPMENT LIST

ITEM NO.	DESCRIPTION	SERIAL NO.	MODEL NO.
01	Sanyo – Transcribing Equipment	H4402252	TRC-8080
02	Sanyo – Transcribing Equipment	P7507688	TRC-8080
03	Sanyo – Dictating/Transcribing Equipment	H4501285	TRC-8800
04	Sanyo – Transcribing Equipment	H4402250	TRC-8080
05	Sanyo – Transcribing Equipment	H4402251	TRC-8080
06	Sanyo – Transcribing Equipment	H4402512	TRC-8080
07	Sanyo – Dictating/Transcribing Equipment	P7302789	TRC-8800
08	Sanyo – Transcribing Equipment	H4402249	TRC-8080
09	Sanyo – Transcribing Equipment	P7507771	TRC-8080
10	Sanyo – Transcribing Equipment	P7507770	TRC-8080

Instructions:

1   *Create labels for Olympus foot pedals.*
2   *Save as Labels1.*
3   *Print Labels1.*

AT: #01 Footpedal: Olympus Footswitch: Model RS28 EI:BZ8207-01 **Bar Code: 6298**	**AT: #02** Footpedal: Olympus Footswitch: Model RS28 EI:BZ8207-01 **Bar Code:6300**
AT: #03 Footpedal: Olympus Footswitch: Model RS28 EI:BZ8207-01 **Bar Code: 7591**	**AT: #04** Footpedal: Olympus Footswitch: Model RS28 EI:BZ8207-01 **Bar Code: 7592**
AT: #05 Footpedal: Olympus Footswitch: Model RS28 EI:BZ8207-01 **Bar Code: 7593**	**AT: #06** Footpedal: Olympus Footswitch: Model RS28 EI:BZ8207-01 **Bar Code: 7594**
AT: #07 Footpedal: Olympus Footswitch: Model RS28 EI:BZ8207-01 **Bar Code: 7596**	**AT: #08** Footpedal: Olympus Footswitch:Model RS28 EI:BZ8207-01 **Bar Code: 7597**
AT: #09 Footpedal: Olympus Footswitch: Model RS28 EI:BZ8207-01 **Bar Code: 7598**	**AT: #10** Footpedal: Olympus Footswitch: Model RS28 EI:BZ8207-01 **Bar Code: 7599**

Instructions:

1 *Create labels for Olympus headsets.*
2 *Save as Labels2.*
3 *Print Labels2.*

AT: #01 **Stereo Headset E102: Olympus** **E1-3154-03**	**AT: #02** **Stereo Headset E102: Olympus** **E1-3154-03**
AT: #03 **Stereo Headset E102: Olympus** **E1-3154-03**	**AT: #04** **Stereo Headset E102: Olympus** **E1-3154-03**
AT: #05 **Stereo Headset E102: Olympus** **E1-3154-03**	**AT: #06** **Stereo Headset E102: Olympus** **E1-3154-03**
AT: #07 **Stereo Headset E102: Olympus** **E1-3154-03**	**AT: #08** **Stereo Headset E102: Olympus** **E1-3154-03**
AT: #09 **Stereo Headset E102: Olympus** **E1-3154-03**	**AT: #10** **Stereo Headset E102: Olympus** **E1-3154-03**

Instructions:

1   Type the letter using the standard layout below and set it up to accommodate mail merge.
2   Send this letter to the following recipients:
    Mr John Clarke, Comtech Ltd, Dawson Street, Athenry, Co. Galway.
    Ms Ann Tobin, Super Media Ltd, Shop Street, Athenry, Co. Galway.
    Mr Jim Newell, JN Electronics Ltd, Main Street, Tuam, Co. Galway.
    Mr Pat Donovan, Donovan Bros Ltd, Eglington Street, Oranmore, Co. Galway.
3   Run spell check.
4   Save as Mail merge letter1.
5   Print Mail merge letter1 and address labels for envelopes.

Sender's Letterhead

St John's Education Centre **Slane Street, Athenry, Galway**

Type today's date

   <<Title>>   <<First Name>>   <<Last Name>>
   <<Company Name>>
   <<Address Line 1>>
   <<Town>>
   <<County>>

Dear   <<Title>>   <<Last Name>>

WORK EXPERIENCE

We would be most grateful if you can accommodate our student for a period of work placement, working one day per week in your organisation/business from October 20XX to April 20XX.

Work experience is a requirement for the FETAC Certificate in Business and Marketing Studies. As you can appreciate, it is of great benefit to the students to gain useful work experience in your business.

Some of the modules studied by the students include:

- Customer Service
- Communications
- Spreadsheets
- Databases
- Information Systems
- Marketing
- Internet
- Book-keeping (both manual and computerised)

The college provides insurance cover for the students during the period of work experience.

At the end of the work experience I would be grateful if you could fill out the enclosed Supervisor's Report Form detailing the student's performance for the duration of the work experience.

If you need to clarify anything with me, feel free to email me at any time at joseph.gallagher@yahoo.co.uk or phone me at 085-2344245.

Yours sincerely

_____

Joseph Gallagher
Course Co-ordinator

Instructions:

1. Type the letter using the standard layout below and set it up to accommodate mail merge.

2. Send this letter to the following recipients:

   Ms Anne Ruane, Human Resources Manager, Electrofile Ltd, Abbey Street, Ennis, Co. Clare.

   Ms Jane Walshe, Human Resources Manager, Screen Drive Ltd, Dukes Street, Oranmore, Co. Galway.

   Mr John O'Connor, Human Resources Manager, First Call Direct Ltd, Fair View, Castlebar, Co. Mayo.

   Mr Paul Fitzgibbon, Human Resources Manager, Domnick Street, Ballina, Co. Mayo.

3. Run spell check.

4. Save as Mail merge Letter2.

5. Print Mail merge letter2 and address labels for envelopes.

Sender's Letterhead

Ms Sandra Broderick
Main Street
Castlebar
Co. Mayo

Type today's date

<<Title>>   <<First Name>>   <<Last Name>>
<<Company Name>>
<<Address Line 1>>
<<Town>>
<<County>>

<<Dear>>   <<Title>>   <<Last Name>>

I wish to be considered for any suitable secretarial position that may arise within your company. I am a highly qualified secretary, with 60 wpm in typing, audio transcription skills and high standards of precision and accuracy. I have ten years' experience in the industry. I am also fluent in Irish and French.

Enclosed please find my curriculum vitae, together with reference contact numbers.

I appreciate the time you have taken to review my details and I look forward to hearing from you.

Yours sincerely

_____
Sandra Broderick
Enc